T0277228

SCALING SMART

SCALING SMART

HOW TO DESIGN
A SELF-MANAGING BUSINESS

RICH FETTKE AND KATHY FETTKE

BiggerPockets®
PUBLISHING
Denver, Colorado

Scaling Smart: How to Design a Self-Managing Business
Rich Fettke and Kathy Fettke

Published by BiggerPockets Publishing LLC, Denver, CO
Copyright © 2024 by Rich Fettke and Kathy Fettke
All rights reserved.

Publisher's Cataloging-in-Publication Data
Names: Fettke, Rich, author. | Fettke, Kathy, author.
Title: Scaling smart : how to design a self-managing business / by Rich Fettke and Kathy Fettke.
Description: Includes bibliographical references. | Denver, CO: BiggerPockets Publishing LLC, 2024.
Identifiers: LCCN: 2024939369 | ISBN: 9781960178169 (hardcover) | 9781960178176 (ebook)
Subjects: LCSH Small business--Growth. | Small business--Management. | Strategic planning. | Entrepreneurship. | Real estate business. | BISAC BUSINESS & ECONOMICS / Entrepreneurship | BUSINESS & ECONOMICS / Small Business | BUSINESS & ECONOMICS / Investments & Securities / Real Estate | BUSINESS & ECONOMICS / Real Estate / General
Classification: LCC HD62.7 .F46 2024 | DDC 658.4/06--dc23

Printed on recycled paper in Canada
FR 10 9 8 7 6 5 4 3 2 1

DEDICATION

*To all you brave entrepreneurs out there—this one's for you.
Your courage, grit, and passion light up the path for making
a real difference in the world. Your stories and struggles are the
heart and soul behind every word we've written.*

*A huge shout-out to everyone at RealWealth for being the dream team.
Your dedication is the magic that fuels our purpose to help people build
real, lasting wealth. Each of you is a key player in this adventure, and
we couldn't have done it without your hard work and creativity.
Remember, "The only thing more important than a great idea is the
team that can see it through!" This rings true for us every day. It's all
about sticking together and pushing forward, turning our big dreams
into reality.*

*Here's to all of us who are chasing dreams, making a dent in the
universe, and building something truly great together.
Let's keep this incredible journey going!*

TABLE OF CONTENTS

PART III
IT'S ABOUT THE PEOPLE

PART IV
LET'S GET NERDY (SCALING WITH SYSTEMS AND TECHNOLOGY)

INTRODUCTION

Hey there, fellow entrepreneurial spirit! We're thrilled you've picked up this book, because it's not just any book—it's a road map to transforming your business from a time-sucking, stress-inducing monster into a well-oiled, income-generating machine. Picture it: more free time, more money, more impact. Sound too good to be true? Well, it's not!

We're Rich and Kathy Fettke, a husband-and-wife entrepreneur team, and we're going to show you how it's done.

Now, before you start thinking this is some kind of get-rich-quick scheme, you need to know this book isn't about finding some magical unicorn of a business idea or riding the latest fad to a quick buck. No, this is about creating sustainable, passive income by building a business that can run on autopilot while still making a difference in the world.

It doesn't matter what kind of business you run. Maybe you're selling a service or product. Maybe you're a broker, real estate investor, wholesaler, flipper, self-storage operator, owner of several mobile home parks, or syndicator of multifamily or commercial real estate deals.

What matters is that you are entrepreneurial—you want to build something great and have the money and the freedom to live life on your terms. You want to make a difference in the lives of your family and all the people your business serves. You don't want to be told what to do or when to do it, or that you can't do something.

We understand. As entrepreneurs, we think differently. We know what it's like to be in the trenches, working long hours and feeling like you're going to drown in a sea of never-ending tasks. Many entrepreneurs start out with a goal to create freedom, yet they end up spending every waking moment working in their business. Sometimes it seems they've left the 9-to-5 world only to find themselves in the 24/7 world!

Running a business is much more difficult than most people will tell you. It takes courage, faith, focus, effort, and sometimes pain. Some days, you're feeling great; others, you consider throwing in the towel. However, if you stay in the fight and continue to learn and grow, the rewards are worth it. We are here to help you with that.

Since you're reading this book, you probably want to expand your business. Maybe you have worked out a lot of the kinks and things are running more smoothly than when you started. But you're feeling stagnant, like you've hit a ceiling. You want to grow your business, but before you do, you've got to make sure you have a solid foundation in place to handle growth.

We don't want you to do what too many entrepreneurs do: try to grow too quickly. We've seen countless friends and colleagues get caught up in the narrative of explosive business growth, trying to "10x their business" in a year. Often, the only explosions are the overwhelm, frustration, confusion, and meltdowns that happen with their employees and customers. They end up spending so much time and money trying to grow their business quickly that they end up growing themselves broke. According to the U.S. Bureau of Labor Statistics, 45 percent of businesses fail within five years, and 65 percent fail within ten years.[1] We don't want you to become a statistic.

That's why we wrote this book—to guide you, step by step, on automating your business the smart way, taking the right steps at the right time, and not growing yourself broke. We've been where you are, and that's why we're so excited to share our journey to business freedom with you.

KATHY'S STORY

I am a true entrepreneur: I have lots of business ideas, and I'm great at putting them into action. I get flooded with ideas for ways to make money on just about anything. If there's a need, I want to fill it and profit from it.

I started my first "business" in the '80s when I was in high school. My dad planted a garden that produced way more fruit and vegetables than we could eat. We decided to start a farm-to-table restaurant in

---

[1] "Business Employment Dynamics," U.S. Bureau of Labor Statistics, April 28, 2016, https://www.bls.gov/bdm/entrepreneurship/entrepreneurship.htm.

our backyard, inviting neighbors and friends to $20 luncheons where they could also learn how to garden and cook. It was a great learning experience on how to market and sell a unique service. And more importantly, I learned that I had to count the cost of my time in addition to the business expenses. With the amount of time I was spending on this project, I realized I was ultimately working for free.

Later, during college, I had a job selling acting classes to aspiring actors and earned a nice percentage of each sale. But I soon found out I was working for a con artist, so I quit and decided to start my own acting school—a legitimate one, taught by the largest casting director in San Francisco. That led me to start a new business—a talent agency—so my students could land roles in commercials and TV shows.

What I didn't learn in these ventures was how to grow my business beyond myself. I was the one running everything. I had no idea how to hire people to help me, and when I tried, it ended up creating more work for me. I had to start working at dawn and end late at night just to keep up.

Then I met Rich and it changed everything. When I had to cancel most of our dates to tend to my business, I realized it was time for me to find a way to have a life.

I sold the talent agency for a pittance. Had I created systems and structures, I could have kept it or sold it for a large sum. Nobody wants to buy a one-person show; they want to buy a business that runs on its own. Case in point: The casting director, who had become a good friend of mine, was a master of delegation. His company was so well-run and systematized, he was freed up to work on ways to improve it. At the time, casting directors had filing cabinets full of actors' headshots, which had to had to be reviewed manually. He developed the first online portal to make the selection process easier, and he sold that company for millions of dollars. I watched him build it in just a few years, and I even lent him the $4,000 he needed to get it started. (I should have asked for an equity position!)

After walking away from my talent agency for practically nothing, I followed my dream of being in the news business and went to work at ABC, Fox, and CNN. After working for myself, I was craving regular work hours. But I soon found out I had no control over my schedule; my hours were long and varied wildly.

By that point, Rich and I were married, and I soon became pregnant. Rich's career in business coaching had taken off, and there was plenty of money, so I was able to be a stay-at-home mom.

Life was blissful—until the day Rich received a fatal skin cancer diagnosis and was told he had maybe six months to live. Despite the emotional shock of this news, I decided it was time to get back to work, so Rich could focus on his health. But I wanted to work from home, so I could be with my family during this difficult time.

I'd heard about "passive income" yet had no idea how to make it. I didn't know any wealthy people or anyone who was earning passive income, so I started reading books about it.

Luckily, I had continued hosting a weekend radio show for fun and to keep myself connected to the industry. I began interviewing the authors of my favorite books, along with other millionaires, so I could learn their secrets about money. I noticed a common theme: They had all amassed great wealth through *owning businesses that essentially ran themselves.* They would take the profits from their businesses and invest them in more cash-flowing assets, like real estate.

To help with our cash flow needs during this challenging time, I found a mortgage broker who agreed to sponsor the show. To keep it interesting, I decided to interview his clients to see what they were doing with those loans. That's when both my audience and I learned the power of leverage in building a real estate portfolio: basically using very little of one's own money to acquire cash-flowing assets. The show took off, and our phones started ringing off the hook with people who wanted a mortgage to buy an income-producing property. The response was more than my sponsor could handle, so he urged me to get my real estate license and join his firm. I soon became one of the busiest mortgage brokers in the San Francisco Bay Area.

Then, a miracle happened: It turned out the skin cancer had not spread to Rich's liver, as the doctor originally thought. Hallelujah! He was able to get it all removed and could get back to speaking and coaching.

We took what I was learning from all those real estate millionaires on my show and began to invest in rental properties. When I spoke about our investments on the radio show, our phones started ringing off the hook again with people who wanted to do the same.

In addition to getting loans from me, my listeners wanted to know who I was using for my real estate broker, property management, insurance, asset protection, and taxes. Soon, it became clear that there was a great need for a real estate investment company to help people build rental portfolios in the fastest-growing cities in the country. That's when the RealWealth network was born. We helped hundreds of our members buy properties out of state through our network of experts.

Word got out about the great returns we were getting outside of California, so I started to get invited to speak at local real estate investor associations (REIAs). All the while, my *Real Wealth Show* audience continued to grow. I felt like I was in a fast car that I didn't know how to drive, and I didn't know how to slow down. It was exciting and I loved it, but it was also scary and exhausting.

I didn't know how to hire help, so instead I took on a partner to help me. Unfortunately, I didn't require that he buy in; I just gave him half the business and thought he'd take on half the work. This was not the case. Instead, I found myself working harder while having to split the company's income.

By 2008, the Great Recession was starting, and I was ready to give up. Banks were failing. Property values were tanking. Foreclosures were ticking up into the millions, and builders were going bankrupt. Few people wanted to buy property, and that translated to low demand for mortgages. Business came to a sudden halt.

On top of that, a builder we worked with went bankrupt, leaving dozens of our investors facing the potential loss of their earnest money deposits. I promised them I'd find a way to make it right. At the same time, my business partner and I decided to split. I bought him out for $5,000. And I was left with the expenses that had piled up. Now I was left with a company that could barely pay its bills and no real prospects for bringing in new business.

It would be easy to blame my struggles on the mortgage meltdown or my business partner. The real story is that I didn't know how to run a business. If I had, I wouldn't have taken on a partner and given him 50 percent of my profits without significant capital buy-in. I would have hired people with the specific skills I needed. I would have had better systems for vetting vendors and plenty of reserves set aside for economic downturns.

Then I had a sudden realization: My husband had a business degree, had run several successful businesses, and was a highly sought-after business coach, author, and speaker. Could Rich be my new business partner? Could we get along as business partners? Or would this be unsuccessful too, and I'd have to sell my business for practically nothing—again?

RICH'S STORY

I grew up thinking I'd never amount to anything. When I was 8 years old, the doctor diagnosed me with hyperkinetic disorder (today's ADHD). I was prescribed Ritalin and was put in classes for the "learning disabled" at school.

I had a hard time focusing and despised school. Some of my deficiency reports had a checkbox marked next to "Lacks what it takes to succeed." I even found out late in my senior year that I had to return for summer school if I wanted to get my high school diploma. Believing in myself was not my reality.

I also had to deal with a high school bully who continually beat me up. I decided to protect myself by learning martial arts and lifting weights. This taught me discipline. That discipline started to pay off, and I enrolled in community college and finally learned how to focus, study, and learn.

At age 23, I decided to open a health club in my home state of Massachusetts, with two good friends as business partners and my parents cosigning on the business loan and equipment lease. The first six months were very difficult. Like most new entrepreneurs, we were overly optimistic about our projections. We didn't sign up members as fast as we thought we would, and we still had a lot of operating expenses to cover. I remember the stack of unpaid bills on my desk staring at me, telling me I was going to fail.

About that time, my uncle gave me my first business book, called *The E-Myth*. After that, I grew obsessed with business, goals, sales, and personal growth and started learning from classic mentors like Brian Tracy, Stephen Covey, Tony Robbins, and Zig Ziglar. I began to apply their lessons, and our business went from a pile of unpaid bills to consistently improving profits. We hired more people and trained them on our systems and processes.

Once I completed my associate's degree, I enrolled in business college and learned about accounting, business law, marketing, and how to create a solid business plan with projections, market analysis, and more. After running the health club for seven years and going from three to twenty-four employees, I sold my ownership in the business and moved to California.

About six months later, I met Kathy, and we were married a year and a half later. Over the next several years, I built a thriving coaching business, made big bucks giving keynote speeches at conferences, and signed a six-figure book deal with Simon & Schuster. We had two young daughters and owned a great home that we turned into a triplex by converting the lower level of the home into two small apartments, each with their own entrance. At the same time, the property was rising in value by about $100,000 a year. I felt on top of my game.

That's when my doctor delivered my fatal cancer diagnosis, and I had to step back. Way back.

For the next five years, I helped Kathy with marketing, technology, and much more; she called me her "Chief Support Guy." Meanwhile, I had surgeries to remove the melanoma, and later it turned out my diagnosis wasn't fatal after all. I'd received a "false diagnosis," or what the doctors called a "false positive." They thought the melanoma had spread to my liver, but I was cancer free.

The "curse" of the wrong diagnosis was actually the "blessing" that inspired Kathy to become a mortgage broker with a focus on real estate investing to make ends meet in case I did die. And in 2008, when Kathy and her business partner split, she asked me if I would be willing to partner with her in the business. I said yes.

THE TURNING POINT

We started to focus on building systems, processes, and hiring the right people to help us. It worked for a while, and we were thrilled that our small business broke into the rare $1-million-in-annual-revenue club. But then we got stuck: We hit a plateau of just over $1 million in revenue for the next two years.

Even though Rich already had his bachelor's degree in business, we decided it was time to invest in more business education. We attended a rather expensive weekend workshop for business owners and entrepreneurs, but we knew it would be worth it. And it certainly was. We began to think bigger and operate smarter. We became obsessed with creating a business with an empowered team aligned around our purpose, mission, vision, and values.

In the year after the workshop, we had huge growth as a company, both in how we ran the business and in revenue. RealWealth Network (later shortened to RealWealth) ended up making the Inc. 5000 list that year—and the next two years as well!

Today, we've helped investors acquire more than 7,000 rental properties and over $1.3 billion in assets, and we've syndicated more than a dozen residential developments. We also operate on the principles of conscious capitalism—we donate 10 percent of our profits (we're now up to almost $1 million in total donations) to charitable organizations that change the world.

We've kept our company small but nimble and effective. We have had as many as twenty-seven employees and another dozen independent contractors. Today, our company is made up of about twenty employees, and we work with eighteen different property teams around the country, each with an average of about fifteen employees.

We're not claiming to have scaled billion-dollar businesses. We're simply partners who have learned, bootstrapped, succeeded, failed, picked ourselves up again, learned some more, and built a solid business with a purpose and an amazing team. We're at a place where we have the freedom to trust our team to run things while we travel, focus on passion projects, and spend more time with the people we love.

WHY "SCALING SMART"?

This book is not called *Scaling Fast*. It's also not called *Scaling Big*. The title is *Scaling Smart* for a reason.

Think of your smartphone, smart home, or smart car. These things are all built to be customizable to your individual needs, saving you time, money, and energy. You can put your clothes in a smart washer, and it knows how much water to use based on the size of the load. When you get into your smart car, it knows how you like to sit, when the windshield wipers should go on, and even warns you if you are driving recklessly. And smartphones—well, we all know how those have changed our lives. It's like having a personal assistant, a doctor, a librarian, a scientist … honestly, anything you need, at your fingertips.

Can you imagine what it would be like to have a smart company, customized to serve your schedule, your specific needs, your lifestyle? What if it was smart enough to know how to make decisions that grow the business while also saving you money, time, and energy? What if you could count on it to be consistent like clockwork *and* have the ability to sense what needs improvement, always aware and learning how to be better and more competitive?

That's what happens to your business when you scale smart. And we'll teach you how to do it.

Important note: If you are just starting your business, you should not be focused on scaling yet. You need to first create a business plan that outlines the objectives, strategies, market analysis, financial projections, and operational framework for starting and operating your business. The plan details how your business intends to achieve its goals, including product or service offerings, who your target market is, competitive analysis, marketing and sales strategies, and a detailed financial plan covering revenue projections, budgeting, and cash flow. It will help you evaluate the viability and potential profitability of your business idea before committing money or time. There's a multitude of books and courses on how to create a solid business plan.

This book *is* for you if you're an entrepreneur who has been through some start-up challenges and is now operating a business, serving customers or clients, and making a profit—and is ready to scale into something that will increase your wealth while freeing up your time to focus more on what you're great at and what you love doing.

THE GOAL OF THIS BOOK

We've written this book to share our knowledge with you. It can be difficult to apply the lessons from billion-dollar businesses to a small, growing business. Over the past twenty-plus years, we have created a system that can help any entrepreneur turn their existing company into a self-managing, profitable business. Since our business focus has been real estate investing, we will share several specific examples in this book that can help you scale your real estate business the smart way. However, this system can be applied to any type of company that is ready to scale.

We've also tapped into our network of entrepreneur friends and experts for their pearls of wisdom. The result is a comprehensive guide that covers everything from purpose-driven leadership and effective communication to building self-managing teams and creating systems that set you free.

We've divided this book into four parts. Part I is focused on you. Just like any smart product needs to know user preferences to function well, you have to know what you want from your business (why you want to scale it) so that it can perform optimally. We'll start by discussing why growth and scaling are important for your business, then do a deep dive on you—defining your "why," your idea of wealth, and your personal vision. You'll also get clear on your purpose, mission, and vision for your business.

Part II is focused on your business. What is it really about? What is its core service? The clearer we are on our business purpose, the less likely we are to try to make it do something it wasn't built to do. We'll discuss business structures, systems, and specialists, including topics like organizational charts and outsourcing.

Part III will look at the "people" part of your business: your company's culture, vibe, and values; leadership, training, managing, and inspiring people; and working with partners.

Finally, Part IV is about how to operate your smart business so it becomes so automated you don't have to think about it. It knows what to do and how to do it while continuing to grow and improve. You'll discover how to use technology and other tools to scale your organization and put your business on autopilot.

This book will help you:

- Learn the difference between growth and scaling and why scaling is the key to creating passive income and freeing up your time.
- Understand the dangers of expanding your business too fast and learn how to scale wisely.
- Discover the importance of having a clear personal vision *before* creating a company vision and how it can help you achieve real wealth.
- Develop a smart growth plan, create clear systems and structures, and track key numbers to avoid growing yourself broke.
- Gain practical skills in connecting, training, managing, empowering, and inspiring your team.
- Master the art of personal leadership and effective communication and how to implement conscious capitalism throughout your organization.
- Leverage technology, processes, AI, and tools to get more done with less effort and scale your business efficiently.

Too often, a business can morph into a monster we don't know how to control. In this book, we are going to show you how to tame that monster so it becomes more like a genie: here to serve the wishes of your clients, your team, and you.

You *can* stop being chained to your company and say goodbye to stress and overwhelm. You *can* create a self-managing business that brings you more wealth, freedom, and fulfillment and allows you to make a difference in the world while staying true to your soul and entrepreneurial spirit.

Let's get started!

PART I
LET'S START
WITH YOU

CHAPTER 1

WHY GROW?

If you want success in one to three years, you might be disappointed. Stick with it and be consistent. Getting 1 percent better every week compounds to incredible lengths, but only if you let the compounding progress.

—SCOTT TRENCH, CEO, BIGGERPOCKETS

What would you rather have: a company that earns $10 million and spends $12 million every year or a company that earns $5 million and spends $4 million every year? One company sounds like it's in debt. The other sounds like it has profit, reserves, and funds for further growth.

We like the second company.

Debt is not a bad thing if it helps accelerate your growth and if you have a plan to pay it off with increased revenue. Many business giants like Zillow, Pinterest, and Lyft have been running at a loss for years. But how sustainable is that?

We understand why so many people get ahead of themselves when it comes to growing their businesses. It's tempting to want to be a big shot, and it looks so easy when others are doing it right. Plus, in the business world, "growth" is the big buzzword. If you're not growing, you're dying.

But *sustainable* growth is the key to survival. Business giants like Amazon, Apple, and Berkshire Hathaway have been able to sustain meteoric growth, despite challenges, because they know how to grow and they know how to scale.

GROWTH VS. SCALING: WHAT'S THE DIFFERENCE?

Let's break down the differences between "growth" and "scaling."

Growth: Think of it like this—you put in some resources (money, people, technology), and in return, you get more money. Sounds good, right? But the more you grow, the more resources you need to maintain that growth. For instance, if a real estate brokerage gets more clients, they'll probably need to hire more people. And then the brokerage will need to keep all those clients, or get even more clients, to make enough money to keep everyone employed. Yes, growth is important, but you need to be careful of *how* you grow. We'll talk more about that in this chapter.

Scaling: Now, scaling is where the magic happens—your business makes more money by using cost-effective strategies to scale up. You still grow, but without spending a lot of additional resources (money, people, technology) to achieve this growth. For example, if you send an email to one hundred people, it wouldn't really take much more effort or money to send it to 100,000 people, right? Or if you want to host an event, you could put on a webinar and your costs would be pretty much the same no matter how many people attend. However, if you held the event in person, that would involve a room rental, and your costs would increase as the number of attendees increased.

Both growth and scaling are important, but the trick is knowing when to focus on which. If you only focus on growth for too long, there's a good chance you could end up allocating too much capital and resources trying to constantly up your goal. You might end up growing your business broke.

The Tortoise and the Hare: Regus vs. WeWork

Let's look at two case studies of growth: WeWork and Regus.

WeWork is a great example of a company that took off like a rocket ship. They started with a great idea to build collaborative, more affordable workspaces to support budding entrepreneurs. They grew and grew, and SoftBank invested billions of dollars into the company. The company was valued at $47 billion during its peak in 2019. However, a few months after this valuation, WeWork filed for an IPO. Documents showed that the company was losing $219,000 every hour! The losses skyrocketed in 2020, when the pandemic hit and office spaces were shut down. They still went public in 2021, at a $9 billion valuation, despite the filings showing billion-dollar losses. Not surprisingly, WeWork filed for bankruptcy in 2023.

While you could certainly blame the company's challenges on the pandemic, its competitor Regus has a different story. Regus experienced major losses during the pandemic too, but it was able to bounce back and have even higher returns in 2023 than before the pandemic.

What was the difference?

You could call WeWork the hare. They came out fast and flashy. While coworking spaces weren't new, their "cool" factor, targeting a young, hip demographic was. Investment money poured in, but instead of using it to vertically integrate and improve the core business, WeWork used it to create an array of new businesses: WeLive, WeGrow, Rise by We, WeWork Labs, and WeWork Food Labs. The result: high debt, poor accounting, and contracts that couldn't be fulfilled. They simply tried to do too many things at once, not giving energy and focus to the core business.

Regus, on the other hand, took the tortoise approach. The company is no-frills. You get access to a normal office, a shared conference room, and support from the front desk receptionist. You share the coffee maker, not shots of Don Julio 1942 tequila. While perhaps not as exciting, Regus stuck with the model of providing a place to do business, not throw parties.[2]

You may be wondering if this tortoise-versus-hare debate applies to you if you're not planning to build a multibillion-dollar business. We say it does.

Through the years, we have seen smaller entrepreneurs with great ideas do the same thing: They try to grow too fast by taking on too many expenses and too much debt, only to find themselves cash poor and, eventually, bankrupt or broke. They get cocky before they have experience or a track record, and before their business has been tested against the inevitable ups and downs of life. Not only have we seen others do this time and time again, we've even done it ourselves. It's no fun to have to tell your employees you can't pay them this month when they have mouths to feed at home.

Nothing beats the peace of mind of having reserves. No idea is worth going into debt for if you don't have a clear path to get out of it. And, most importantly, no business or idea is worth taking you away from the things that matter most to you, only to end up worse off than when you started. This is why we are so passionate about helping you take your great idea and scaling it the smart way.

---

2   Sarah Jackson, "'Activate the Space': WeWork Foundeer Adam Neumann Made Staff Sit at Empty Desks, Throw Parties, and Play The Notorius B.I.G. When Investors Toured Buildings, New Book Says," *Business Insider*, July 20, 2021, https://www.businessinsider.com/wework-staff-throw-parties-fill-empty-desks-cult-of-we-2021-7.

THE DANGERS OF GROWING TOO FAST

At business events and on social media, it can feel like everyone's shouting, "Let's 10x this baby!" It's like a viral dance challenge, but for businesses. It can be intoxicating, but it can make you feel like a loser if you're not on the Inc. 5000 list of fastest-growing businesses every year.

We are not knocking the 10x goal. In fact, we've 10xed our own business a few times—and it does feel great to be on the Inc. 5000 list three years in a row! What we're saying is that if you try to 10x without the right systems and processes in place, you could end up in the same place as WeWork—spending more money than you're making and eventually filing bankruptcy to restructure things the way you should have in the first place.

We have been to many events where a newbie comes to us and says, "I want to be a real estate syndicator like you and raise money from investors. How do I do it?" We then ask, "How much experience do you have in real estate?" Oftentimes, we discover they are just starting out. This is a recipe for disaster! Few people can scale a company smartly if they don't really know the business they are in or how to run a business at all.

Seeing new business owners wanting to hit that 10x (or, dare we say, 100x) in a flash worries us like parents hearing their kid say, "I'm going to jump into the deep end of the pool!" when they still don't know how to swim.

Aiming for the stars is cool. But (and it's a big but) you've gotta be real about your timeline. Zooming your business into hyperdrive has its pitfalls. Let's break them down.

OPERATIONAL OVERLOAD

Imagine trying to run a marathon in the same old tennis shoes you've had for the last ten years. That's your old system trying to handle your mega expansion. Rapid expansion can stretch—and break—the capacity of your company's operations. The infrastructure, systems, and processes that worked for your company when it was smaller might not handle the demands of a larger organization.

QUALITY SLIPUPS

Speeding up can sometimes mean slipping up, and the quality of your products or services takes a nosedive. Compromising the quality of your products or services during rapid expansion can upset your loyal customers and mess with your brand's reputation.

TOO MUCH FINANCIAL INVESTMENT

Aggressive scaling can require significant financial investment. But not all of these will give you the returns you dream of, which can sting the wallet. If your risky investments don't provide the anticipated returns, you make your company financially vulnerable.

STRETCHING THE TEAM TOO THIN

Pushing for quick growth can feel like you're all pulling all-nighters, which can lead to burnout and saying unexpected goodbyes to your team members. Rapid growth can strain your team, potentially leading to high turnover rates and challenges in maintaining your company culture.

CULTURE SHIFTS

Remember the vibe when you first started? Rapid growth can bring in new people who might not embody the original values and ethos of your company and jell with that original spark. Maintaining a solid, connected company culture during rapid expansion can be tough.

DEBT DILEMMAS

To fund turbocharged growth, some business owners take on debt or sell parts of the business to raise equity—which can be a dicey game of higher interest payments, reduced profitability, or dilution of ownership for existing shareholders.

CUSTOMER SERVICE ERRORS

More customers can lead to more problems. With a surge in buyers or clients, your company's existing service infrastructure might get overwhelmed, leading to potentially unhappy customers.

DECISION-MAKING BOTTLENECKS

With growth can come the "too many cooks in the kitchen" problem. Making choices might take longer, and not always in a good way. As the company grows, decision-making can become slower or more bureaucratic, impacting agility.

SUPPLY CHAIN OR CONTRACTOR SURPRISES

Growing too fast may mean you'll become more dependent on your current suppliers and contractors, or that you'll need to find new suppliers and contractors to meet your increased demands. This can introduce some major new challenges if your current vendors can't meet your needs, or you can't find suppliers and contractors who can.

EXTERNAL CURVEBALLS

The world's a wild place. Recessions, international drama, and pandemics can throw off your scaling plans. Whether it's an economic downturn, a geopolitical issue, a global health crisis, or something else, unforeseen factors will impact your company. Scale too fast and you won't be prepared to handle these curveballs.

"Speed Kills": Explosive Growth Can Sabotage You

One of the dangers of trying to grow a business too fast occurs when damaging forces beyond your control happen—and sooner or later, they *will* happen.

Brian Scrone had a very successful BRRRR (buy, rehab, rent, refinance, repeat) company in California with about twenty employees. He sold all his properties for top dollar in 2006 and 2007. Then, instead of taking time to breathe and evaluate his options, he plunged right into his next project.

"I was young, and the business had millions of dollars coming in. I wasn't married, I didn't have any children, I was very flexible. I liquidated out of California and plowed millions of dollars into Florida in 2006 and 2007. And then, 2008 happened and I got crushed. I had done our homework; I had identified a market in Jacksonville with sound fundamentals. But [it was] the wrong neighborhood and wrong timing. I was using way too much leverage or debt with the banks. To be candid with you, I should have sat on the sidelines, but I didn't have that crystal ball to show the 2008 crisis looming around the corner.

"There's a saying that 'speed kills.' If I had taken my time, I would have had a ton of breathing room, as much as I needed again. But I grew up around New York City and Wall Street, where it's very fast-paced and very competitive. Like, get out, get after it. That was just part of the way I was raised. Grind, grind it out.

"But now I don't. I am still a huge fan of having a really good work ethic, but now I'm much more of a fan of working smart. And I think there's a healthy hybrid of those two. Once you have a mature business, you can probably work a lot smarter and a lot easier."

Brian learned some valuable lessons, got clear on what's important to him, and decided to scale down. Now, with a wife and kids,

> he wants time for himself and his family. His company is still making plenty of money but with a much smaller staff and the bulk of his team on commission, so the company can scale based on the season.
>
> "I learned a lot about being able to scale and having a good-size team and a good-size portfolio but not a lot of fixed overhead. We are now very conservative with debt, and I have a much smaller portfolio of homes that are low leveraged. Now if there's a downturn, I'm not scrambling."

GROW WISELY, NOT FAST AND FRANTIC

Inch by inch, life's a cinch. Yard by yard, life is hard.

—UNKNOWN

FOMO is real. The fear of missing out got a lot of people in trouble in 2022. Due to low interest rates in 2021, apartment owners were selling their properties for often twice what they'd paid. New investors flocked into the business with the hopes of reaping similar rewards. Unfortunately, for many, they were too late to the game.

In 2022, the Federal Reserve hiked interest rates, bringing the commercial real estate industry to its knees. Anyone on an adjustable-rate mortgage saw their payment more than double, which cut their cash flows in half. One investment group was hit so hard, its bankruptcy filing made headline news in the *Wall Street Journal*: "Houston Apartment Owner Loses 3,200 Units to Foreclosure as Multifamily Feels the Heat."[3] The article goes on to explain how the owners, Applesway Investment Group, had borrowed nearly $230 million to acquire four apartment complexes during the pandemic. But by 2023, the interest rate on those loans had gone way up—one of the properties went from 3.4 percent to 8 percent! Investors lost everything.

It would be easy to blame this failure on the fact that the chief executive of the investment group, Jay Gajavelli, was a new syndicator with only a few years of experience as a multifamily operator. But larger, more experienced firms faced a similar fate. Veritas, a San Francisco–based private equity firm, defaulted on a $448 million loan on their apartment

---

3 Will Parker and Konrad Putzier, "Houston Apartment Owner Loses 3,200 Units to Foreclosure as Multifaimly Feels the Heat," *The Wall Street Journal*, April 11, 2023, https://www.wsj.com/articles/houston-apartment-owner-loses-3-200-units-to-foreclosure-as-multifamily-feels-the-heat-fb3d0e75.

portfolio[4] at about the same time, and the Blackstone Group was negotiating its debt for properties in New York.[5]

Similar companies that had either locked in fixed-rate debt or took on less debt survived the rate hikes, since demand for apartments had not waned. To play the long game, you have to think long term.

The Applesway Investment Group had been very successful on prior projects, due to great timing. They didn't need to take unnecessary risk. Had they slowed down a bit and opted for slower, more sustainable growth, they would be in a cash-rich position instead of bankrupt. Many people in business have a strong desire to grow fast and be "uber successful," but they often don't know why that is their goal, and they end up self-sabotaging like the companies we just mentioned. Before you get caught up in chasing success, make sure you take some time to look at your "why," which we'll discuss more in Chapter 2.

Scaling, One Step at a Time

Kevin B. Rosenbloom is a sports pedorthist and biomechanist who helps patients with foot, leg, hip, and back pain. As CEO of Kevin-Root Medical in Southern California, he empowers clinicians worldwide to help patient performance and outcomes with innovative orthotic and shoe gear technology.

How did he scale from a scrappy start-up to a multimillion-dollar company in just ten years? Kevin says he found success by keeping expenses and debt down and cash reserves up, which allowed him to seize big opportunities when they came along. At age 27, Kevin was a rep for an orthotics company selling custom-made, medical-grade shoe inserts you buy from your doctor. When the company shut down, Kevin went to his doctor clients to see if they would still like to work with him if he opened his own lab. Some said no, but a few said yes. That's all he needed to get started.

He got another sales job to cover his overhead and on the side built a lab to manufacture orthotics. "I decided I'd be the best at one thing," he says.

---

4 Kevin Truong, "San Francisco's Biggest Landlord Defaulted on a Massive Loan," *The San Francisco Standard,* January 13, 2023, https://sfstandard.com/2023/01/13/san-franciscos-biggest-landlord-defaulted-on-a-massive-loan/.

5 Jack Sidders, "Blackstone Reaches Deal With Bondholders on Defaulted Nordic Debt," *Bloomberg,* December 15, 2023, https://www.bloomberg.com/news/articles/2023-12-15/blackstone-reaches-deal-with-bondholders-on-defaulted-nordic-debt.

Kevin didn't have fancy scanning technology, so he rented a garage and bought the basic supplies he needed. He focused on taking great care of each client, which turned into many more referrals. He made it a high-service business, scaling one raving client at a time.

"I wore a suit and tie to doctors' offices, and said, 'Let me make an orthotic for you, doc,' and I'd give him one," Kevin explains. "I'd teach doctors how I did it and how I could help their patients."

He wanted to buy scanning equipment, but it was too expensive. He had befriended a sales tech for a CAD (computer-aided design) technology company, who referred him to a business owner who had already bought all the equipment and now wanted to sell his company. Kevin was able to buy it with money he'd saved, gaining $300,000 worth of equipment for $160,000—plus access to another ten clients.

That's when Kevin learned he could really scale his business by buying other businesses. This could include failed businesses or those from retirees or owners' widows. "I never got a loan, though they're available. I just did cash buys, seller financing, and sometimes took over businesses for a share in profits," he says.

It has been more than twelve years since Kevin opened his lab, and he now works with professional athletes worldwide. He travels the globe to assess materials and technologies, studying with the best of the best to ensure his clients are getting the most premium products and service, and has a top-notch staff helping his company soar.

"I have a twenty-year goal to be the most well-known orthotic company," he says. "I want to help people perform better. I want to work with more professional athletes and team up with doctors of the top athletes in the world."

Meanwhile, Kevin continues to scale his business. "I've had offers over eight figures. But I'm not ready to sell yet. I'm still building."

THE TRAP OF "BIGOREXIA"

Back in the eighties, when I (Rich) had a flowing red mullet and neon baggy pants, I was also a competitive bodybuilder. (Figures, right?) For ten years, I entered competitions ranging from the tiny Salisbury Beach Physique Competition all the way to Mr. Massachusetts (where I placed second). Bodybuilders are not really known for their humility. They can come off as vain and uber confident. They seem like they could be the main characters in an action movie called *Mirror, Mirror on the Wall.* But trust me, beneath those rock-hard pecs and biceps, many of them have a soft, insecure heart pumping, often whispering, "Am I swole enough?" From my experiences and conversations with many of my fellow Arnold Schwarzenegger wannabes, there is often a "not good enough" thought process going on in their minds.

We called it "bigorexia" back in the day—just the opposite of its better-known sister, anorexia. For many bodybuilders, the bigger they get, the more they feel not big enough. Even when others are saying, "Dude, you're looking so buff you're scaring children"—or in the case of my ever-so-delicate Nana, "Rich, you look grotesque"—many bodybuilders can't hear it. Their inner critic's volume? Turned up to eleven.

So rather than walk around in a T-shirt or tank top, people who suffer from bigorexia will wear oversized sweatshirts and baggy pants to try to hide their perceived lack of size. It really is a syndrome that I used to have, along with many of my gym-rat brothers.

Why do I share this? Because now that I've been a business owner for more than thirty-five years and have coached hundreds of business owners and spoken with many more, I've seen that bigorexia can also be a syndrome of entrepreneurs! Nope, it's not about flexing biceps; it's about flexing their business might. No matter how many zeroes are added to their profit, a gnawing thought persists: *Still not enough.* No matter how much growth they experience, there's this belief that it's never enough. (We will discuss ways to battle business bigorexia in Chapter 2.)

UNDERSTANDING YOUR INNER VOICE

What's causing that need to be bigger, faster, and flashier? It could stem from an underlying, deep-seated belief that we don't measure up. A little voice inside our heads, a voice that we may not even be aware of, whispering, "It's true, you aren't enough. No matter how hard you try, I know the truth. You're a loser."

We call this little voice the Gremlin. Many people spend their entire lives trying to prove it wrong. Sometimes they numb it with drugs and alcohol or other addictions. Sometimes they become workaholics to prove they're not losers—chasing status, wealth, and achievement.

Why does the Gremlin exist?

The first eight years of our lives are said to be our most formative years, when our belief systems set in. And let's face it, children aren't always the nicest to each other. Some adults aren't either, for that matter.

For me (Kathy), I was the youngest of five children. I grew up hearing, "You can't play with us. You're not good enough." Or as my sister, who has since apologized on many occasions, would say, "You're ugly. You have buck teeth, so you can't play Miss America with us!"

While I had what most would consider the perfect middle-class upbringing, I still processed these insults as if they were true—even after I got my teeth fixed!

Rich grew up with blazing red hair and freckles. He didn't look like a Ken doll. Add to it that he was hyperkinetic and couldn't pay attention, flunked most classes, and his teachers sent home notices saying he "lacks what it takes to succeed." (Yes, this was allowed in the '70s.) He grew up believing he was ugly and stupid. Now you see why he was working out so hard and getting those spray tans—he wanted to prove the Gremlin wrong.

Unfortunately, our subconscious is way more powerful than our conscious mind. That means no matter how hard we consciously try to overcome our childhood traumas, our subconscious wins every time. That is … until we become conscious of our subconscious.

Remember the monster under our beds that terrified us as children? What happened when we turned on the lights? No Gremlin. Nothing to fear. The same is true of our inner Gremlin. As soon as we shine light on it, it disappears. In other words, the more we can recognize the inner voice criticizing us or scaring us, the less power it has.

Suffice it to say that our addictions to money, power, status, and even drugs stem from old stuff that was thrown at us when we were young and too small to be able to handle it. As we grow up, we can overcome it because we are older, wiser, and more powerful. We just need to be able to hear and recognize that inner voice, so we can have a conversation with it, instead of letting it control us.

Conversations with our inner voice? Sounds crazy, but crazy is what happens when we don't engage and understand where that inner voice comes from. In this book, we hope to help you recognize the voice of the Gremlin, or any other voices that are not authentically yours. We don't want you or your business to be held back.

If you keep listening to that inner critic, you will constantly feel frustrated, overwhelmed, stressed out, and like you are not doing enough. Be careful of your inner critic—don't let it twist your negative thoughts into false beliefs.

FOR THE SAKE OF WHAT?

Years ago, Rich was at a coaching conference where the keynote speaker was a consultant who specialized in working with companies and government agencies to improve their effectiveness as they continued to grow.

The speaker shared a story of how he was hired to work with the elected leaders of a county to help them organize and clarify their annual plan. They told him they were focused on rapid expansion in the next two years by adding new residents and more retail and increasing tax revenue.

He wisely asked the leaders, "For the sake of what?"

That led to hours of discussion around that question. By the end of it, the officials realized they still didn't have a good answer. They eventually decided to ask the residents to vote on what they wanted. The results? The residents wanted a slow growth plan for the county instead.

When you think about your goals and vision for your business, you must ask yourself: For the sake of what? Why do I want this? Why is this important to me? What difference will this make for my customers or clients?

Once you get that perfect answer (because you do know the answer, deep down), ask yourself the following questions to get some clarity on your business growth plan:

1. What's the rush? Why do I need to achieve this goal by a specific date?
2. What will I have to say no to if I say yes to this?
3. How is this in alignment with my values and my purpose?

Here's an example of how to use these questions to find clarity.

Rich came to one of our leadership meetings with an idea. He had met someone at a mastermind who offered mindset coaching to people who weren't ready or able to invest in real estate. This coach told Rich he would pay our company 30 percent of any revenue he earned if we referred clients.

"For the sake of what?" asked Amy, our director of marketing. She had been well trained to ask this question and was also the one who usually ended up saddled with more responsibilities whenever a new idea needed to be implemented.

Rich replied that only about 20 percent of our members at RealWealth are able to invest in property, so this program could help the other 80 percent.

"Do we need to do this now? Is there any rush?" Amy asked.

"No, not really," Rich replied.

"Okay, when would you want this done, and what would I have to say no to if I say yes to this?" she asked. She was already booked solid with initiatives from our quarterly goal-planning meeting.

That's when Michael, our director of finance, jumped in. "Hey, wait, aren't we reading *10x Is Easier Than 2x,* by Dan Sullivan, right now? He said to focus on the 20 percent of our business that brings in the most results. Isn't that where we want to focus, versus the 80 percent of our members who aren't as engaged?"

Rich laughed. "Well done! You're right. You all have done your homework so well. We will scale much faster if we focus on our core business and give excellent service to the people who want what we offer. If we scatter our attention, we can't be as great at the main thing that we are known for: simplifying the process of investing for busy professionals."

Next time you or someone on your team has a brilliant idea they want to tackle, before jumping in, be sure they consider how it will affect the other initiatives already underway. At RealWealth, we put all our new ideas through the BOA, which we'll discuss in Chapter 9.

For the visionaries and dreamers out there, you may want to work with someone to help you answer these questions. I (Kathy) am lucky enough to be married to an experienced business coach, so I am constantly challenged on my never-ending desire to grow.

Whenever I have a new idea or a new project I want to take on, Rich will ask me the questions above. Often, it becomes clear the new ideas are not supportive of the goals we already set and would be distracting to the teams. This doesn't mean the idea gets thrown out. It just gets added to the wish list of things to do, which can be discussed at the next quarterly goal-planning session. That way, the team can make sure an idea fits into the big picture of what we want and what our clients need.

The Entrepreneurial Virus

Dan Coleman, our business coach, is a strategic guide and leadership team coach who helps companies perform better. In the past ten years, he's coached more than seventy companies, with revenues ranging from $3 million to $350 million. He works with growth-minded entrepreneurs who are very coachable and willing to invest in their team and do the work.

One problem he often sees is something he calls the "entrepre-neurial virus."

"It's entrepreneurs who can't decide between what they *should* be doing and what they *could* be doing," he says. "This is a hugely critical point, because entrepreneurs are like hammers looking for a nail. Just because we can be doing something doesn't mean we should be doing something. That's a critical point a lot of entre-preneurs miss. I know there are always budgets in mind, but the entrepreneurs that go big and get the best results are focused on the who, not the how. You've got to fight the entrepreneurial virus of thinking you can do it. Because, to quote Seth Godin, 'Busy is not the point.'"

LET'S BE CLEAR: WE LOVE GROWTH!

Just to clarify, we're not trying to be downers or rain on anyone's parade. We're super passionate about businesses that bring positive change and truly light up your spirit. We just think it's worth mentioning that speed-ing things up too much can sometimes backfire. We hate to see anyone feeling overwhelmed or facing setbacks. Slow and steady often wins the race and can make the race more fun, full of joy, and lucrative. Growing our business has brought amazing results for us. But we also discovered along the way that growing too fast without the right systems in place can bring lots of pain. We want to help you avoid that.

So, what's the play here? It's simple: Plan, reassess, and double-check that growth timeline of yours. Going big is awesome, but do it at a pace that doesn't throw you off track or starve your entrepreneurial soul.

CREATING A GROWTH PLAN

Do you have a growth plan for your business?

Every January at RealWealth, we look at where we'd like to be in three years and then in ten years. Three years is easier to imagine; ten years can feel like a stretch. But that ten-year goal is what can really get the team excited. For example, in our inaugural ten-year-plan meeting, our team came up with a goal to give $1 million to charity through profits and to help our members acquire over $1 billion in real estate investments. Ten years later, we are almost there! While it was a stretch and we haven't quite made it yet, we wouldn't have come close without this plan.

Here are some things to consider when coming up with your growth plan:

- Who's your target market? Has it changed since you last planned or since you started your business?
- How are you best serving them? How can you do more of it and take it to the next level?
- What is your competition doing, and how is your company different?
- What have you been able to accomplish successfully in the past?
- What are some new opportunities your business could pursue that align with your core business focus?
- What are some obstacles/threats/risks that could challenge this plan?
- What do you see as income/cash flow from this new plan?
- What added costs do you anticipate?
- Who can help you get the word out about your awesome product or service?

Note that this plan will change over time as your business grows. You can attack the plan with quarterly goals and then reevaluate your current growth plan once a year, making changes to ensure your plan reflects where you are in your business.

Scaling for Real Estate

Elaine and Nick Stageberg of Black Swan Real Estate scaled their real estate portfolio from one rental to more than 1,200 units in just ten years.

In 2014, they had saved enough money to buy their first fixer-upper. It was after the housing collapse of 2008, and properties were still relatively cheap, especially in Oklahoma City where they lived. They bought a foreclosure for just $35,000 but only had $15,000 left for renovations, so they chose to use their credit cards to cover additional costs.

They were all in at $65,000, but the property appraised for $100,000. They were able to do a cash-out refinance at an 80 percent loan-to-value and get all their money back, pay off their credit card balances, and still have an extra $15,000 in profit. That's the day they realized they needed to do this over and over again.

***NOTE: It is important to evaluate your own finances and credit score before making a decision to use credit cards in lieu of cash.

Then they discovered the power of leverage to scale their real estate business. After moving to Rochester, Minnesota, they bought an old duplex in need of repair for $125,000. They hired handypeople to help them get the renovations done faster, and the duplex appraised for $250,000. Again, they did a cash-out refinance and got all their money back, plus more. After doing a few more of what is now called a BRRRR (buy, rehab, rent, refinance, repeat), they'd built a small team of handymen and created relationships with roofers, plumbers, and HVAC technicians.

They needed money for more deals to keep growing, so they began securing loans from friends, family, and coworkers. Nick got his real estate license so they could look at properties at night after work, have access to available properties they didn't know about before, and keep the commissions they had been paying to agents.

Their small pool of private lenders grew to $1 million, and their rental portfolio blossomed to thirty-five properties. It became clear they could no longer manage everything themselves. They started a property management company to manage their growing portfolio and began hiring contractors, then employees. Elaine and Nick could focus on what they were good at and let others do what they were good at.

They scaled again by managing multifamily properties along with their single-family properties. When they learned that small multifamily properties weren't that different to manage than single-family properties, they reached out to their private lending partners and asked if they wanted to do joint ventures instead of lending.

Hiring the right team and becoming deeply vertically integrated also helped them scale. Instead of using other companies, they hired their own maintenance teams, cleaners, snow clearers, landscapers, and trash removers.

In 2021, they found a ninety-five-unit building for a great price. However, they needed much more money up front to both acquire and renovate the units than could easily be raised through a small joint venture. It was time to look at syndicating.

A real estate syndication is a group of investors who acquire assets together, managed by the general partners.

Elaine and Nick decided to set up their first private equity fund in the same way they had structured their joint ventures: with no general-partner-level fees, all profits first going to return investors' capital, and a 50/50 split thereafter. Syndicating became a reality for them. They grew from a few hundred units to over a thousand in just a few years.

Sometimes, scaling means not taking external action. When multi-family prices peaked in 2023 and interest rates also spiked, inventory in Elaine and Nick's target markets dried up and acquisitions ceased. Instead of trying to make the numbers work, like so many other operators did at the time, Black Swan Real Estate focused on improving their internal systems and processes, so they could operate their buildings as efficiently and profitably as possible. This was the year they expanded their vertical integration into cleaning, lawn care, snow removal, and minor landscaping. By 2024, when multifamily prices came down—as much as 30 percent in some areas—they had new and improved processes and were ready to get back into acquisition mode. Today, they have fifty full-time employees in Rochester and nine virtual assistants.

Elaine attributes their staggering scale in a relatively short period of time to the following principles:

"First, you must have a vivid vision of the future. See your goals as though they have already happened, and then work your way backward. Second, always remember that your number one job is to create massive value. As your journey unfolds, this changes in scope: In the beginning, it was hustling, doing sweat equity renovations ourselves, and taking big risks on distressed properties, and today, it's working with investors, building, training, and leading teams, and understanding both micro- and macroeconomics to guide the portfolio. Finally, real estate will always be a team sport. Your job is to find A+ players who have goals aligned with yours and bring together their talents and resources so that the sum is greater than its parts—contractors, property managers, investors. As the leader, your job is to go back to point number one: Cast a vivid vision of the future and show everyone how their contributions move you all toward that compelling future."

CREATING A SCALING PLAN

We've talked about growing your business, and in the next two chapters, we'll discuss creating personal and business visions. In Parts II, III, and IV of this book, we are going to focus on how to consistently, wisely, and methodically *scale* your business with an emphasis on helping you achieve those visions. We'll make sure you have your systems down, that you know how to create smooth communication within your company, that you know how to grow leaders who can scale, and that you'll be more prepared when opportunities present themselves.

We will also discuss some of the key tips for scaling your business effectively, such as:

- How to cherish your culture: With more people, it's easy for your company's core values to get lost. We will go over how to not let that happen.
- The importance of ditching the tiny tasks: If you're aiming big, focus on the big, important stuff. Delegate or ditch the rest.
- How to create systems and processes: If you've got a routine for something, write it down or create a video. Make it digital. Make sure anyone can pick it up without needing a demo.

It's too early to make a scaling plan for your business now, as the rest of this book will provide you with the information you need to create one. For now, we want you to focus on absorbing the information in the next chapters so you can learn how to scale smart.

TAKEAWAYS

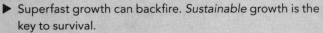

- ▶ Superfast growth can backfire. *Sustainable* growth is the key to survival.
- ▶ Growth involves putting more resources (money, people, technology) into your business to make more money. Scaling involves using cost-effective strategies to scale up your business—still growing but without spending a lot of additional resources to do it.
- ▶ Both growth and scaling are important. The trick is knowing when to focus on which. If you only focus on growth for too long, you could end up allocating too much capital and resources trying to constantly up your goal.
- ▶ Be realistic about your growth timeline.
- ▶ Beware the trap of "bigorexia," where no matter how much growth you experience, it never feels like enough. Keep your ego in check and stop listening to that inner critic.

▶ Think about your business goals and vision and then ask yourself: For the sake of what? Use your answers as a springboard to get clarity on your business growth plan.
▶ Create a growth plan for your business.

CHAPTER 2
SUSTAINABLE GROWTH BEGINS WITH YOU

A human being, like a business, makes profits and suffers losses. For a human being, however, the ultimate currency is not money, nor is it any external measure, such as fame, fortune, or power. The ultimate currency for a human being is happiness. Money and fame are subordinate to happiness and have no intrinsic value. The only reason money and fame may be desirable is that having them or the thought of having them could lead to positive emotions or meaning. In themselves, wealth and fame are worthless: there would be no reason to seek fame and fortune if they did not contribute, in some way, toward happiness.

—TAL BEN-SHAHAR, AUTHOR, *HAPPIER*

As entrepreneurs, we are driven. We are willing to passionately work endless hours to get the job done. We can be competitive, striving to be the best at what we do. We often want recognition for the work we've done—perhaps for the way we've re-created our industry or how we've changed the lives of others. We educate ourselves and learn how to create the best businesses possible. Once we expand our companies, we start reading a few business books that help us get our employees to be as motivated and dedicated as we are. We learn that we can do this by painting a clear vision of where we're headed, one that is so exciting that our teams are fully on board.

Still, there might be something missing in all of this.

That something may be *you*.

You may have a clear vision of where you want your company to go. But do you have a clear vision for where *you* want to go? Do you understand exactly how your business will serve your personal goals?

Do you *have* personal goals? By that, we mean goals that are unrelated to your business, such as how much time you want to spend with your family, where you want to travel, what you want your future net worth to be, or what your lifestyle looks like.

As entrepreneurs, we tend to design our entire lives around our businesses. Our families, our friends, our health, our spirituality, and all the other things that are important to us often take a back seat. That's not because we value these things less, but because we simply don't know how to fit them in when we're doing the heavy lifting of building a business. In our minds, we're doing it all to create a better life for ourselves and our loved ones. In reality, our mental, physical, and spiritual energy is spent almost entirely on business.

In this book, we hope to shift that and help you make your business work for *you,* rather than you working for *it.*

The way to begin is to get crystal clear on your values. We've found that entrepreneurs often haven't taken the time to really investigate this before launching their businesses or trying to scale them. We can assure you that without living by a clear personal vision, your business will take over your life and *become* your life.

It all starts with knowing what you really want. Because if you don't know what you really want, you won't be building a business that gets you there. You'll most likely find yourself burned out, frustrated, and having a midlife crisis. We know too many business owners who have followed the unhealthy path of grinding away to make more money, only to discover that more money did not bring them more fulfillment.

KATHY'S "WHY"

While I (Kathy) was working a nine-to-five job, it felt like a team sport to get to work on time. Unfortunately, the team didn't often play to win. By the time I got the kids up, fed, dressed, and out the door to school, there were only a few moments left for me to get ready and on the road to the office. If there was traffic, I was doomed.

One day, when I felt like I was in the Super Bowl of getting the kids to school, I came up short and was late to work. When I walked in at 9:10 a.m., disheveled and exhausted, the office manager looked at me with her perfectly coiffed hair and makeup, slowly looked down at her watch, and then looked back at me with disgust. I remember thinking, *You don't own me!*

And then I remembered that she did, at least from 9 a.m. to 5 p.m. That's when my "why" became very clear—I wanted to be the owner of my time.

Freedom of time became my most important value. I wanted to be in control of my schedule. I wanted to be able to pick up my kids after school, help them with their homework, make them dinner, and go to their recitals and sporting events. I wanted to be able to work when it fit into my lifestyle.

My second "why" was that I never wanted to be in a situation where I was dependent on someone else for money. When Rich was diagnosed with melanoma, he couldn't take much time off because he was only paid when he worked. I wanted to be financially independent and make sure our basic living expenses would be covered, no matter what. I didn't want to worry about it anymore.

Third, I wanted to be able to live life on my terms. That meant easily affording to send my kids to college; being able to take care of my aging parents and spoil them with vacations they never got to take; not stressing at restaurants when friends ordered expensive meals and then suggesting we evenly split the check.

And last, but not least, I wanted to make a difference. I wanted to leave a legacy—something that would make this world a better place because I was in it.

For Rich and me, our "why" is about squeezing every drop out of life. It means crafting something valuable, embracing growth, and collaborating with a team that's all in on a shared mission. It's also about family. We want our family to have a life overflowing with abundance—in experiences, in generosity, and in love. And now, in our sixth decade of life, we are grateful to say we've achieved just that.

While many people, like me, ditch the nine-to-five to work for themselves in the hopes they will have more control over their time, the opposite often happens. The demands of running a business do not fall within the neat hours of a typical workday, and business owners often find themselves working early in the morning, late at night, and on weekends.

The dream of freedom becomes a distant memory as the emails pile up and the list of to-dos that you don't know how to do grows out of control, like the streets of New York during a garbage strike. We work ourselves ragged—not for a greedy, selfish boss, but for our overwhelmed selves that don't know how to slow down the train.

That is what happened to me when I started working for myself. I was gone more than I was home, and I missed a lot of precious family moments. This was the opposite of what I set out to do. And oddly enough, I wasn't on the treadmill because I needed more money—I was making more money than I ever made as an employee. I was running myself into the ground because I had forgotten *why* I started the business in the first place. I had to remember what it was that I really wanted, and I had to reset to make that the priority.

Rich and I aren't here to tell you how to build a billion-dollar business. We don't own one, and if that's what you want, there are plenty of business books to help you with that. We are here to show you how to take your life back while also owning a thriving business that runs with or without you. We can show you how to replace yourself with people who do most of the work as well as or even better than you, so you can focus your efforts on the parts of the business that you love. We want you to know you can retire—not from your work or your business, but from the parts of it that drain you, so you're free to shine in your areas of expertise that got the business off the ground in the first place.

And most importantly, so you can once again focus on your priorities—whatever they are. And that, of course, means remembering what they are. If you are a left-brain analyst, you may want to skip the next section and get to all the how-to parts of the book. But we urge you to stop and take the time to finish this section.

WHAT IS YOUR PERSONAL "WHY?"

Why are you reading this book? For real. Pause for a moment and give that some thought. You picked up this book for a reason. Answering that question can give you insight into your "why."

Do you want to 10x your business over the next couple of years? Grow a business that brings you enough money to live your dream life? What is your dream life? How much money do you need to live it?

Do you have a strong desire to build something that makes a difference in the world? What is it?

Are you looking for freedom? Freedom to do what? What does freedom look like for you?

There's an ancient Greek term, *telos*, that means having an end goal or purpose in life. Think of it as the ultimate reason you do something or why something exists. Humans are teleological beings; every action we take is pointed toward achieving some kind of end goal, or telos.

When we make decisions, we're figuring out the steps to reach that goal. And if we zoom out, the big-picture goal for most of us is happiness and general well-being (or, as the Greeks called it, *eudaimonia*). Different philosophies put forth different ideas about what this happiness looked like; for example, some believed it was all about pleasure, while others thought it was helping others or living in harmony with nature.

What does happiness look like for you? Think of a time in your life when you felt the most fulfilled and joyful. What was present in your life at the time? What goals were you working toward? As Dr. Ben-Shahar stated in the quote at the beginning of this chapter, happiness is the ultimate currency, and knowing you are moving toward your most important goals is a proven way to create more happiness in your life.

In a nutshell, having a goal or purpose—that telos, aka your "why"— is central to being happy and fulfilled in life. Take a moment now to give your "why" some thought.

What's coming up for you? Please take a moment and make a mental note. Better yet, write it down! Studies show that people who write down their goals have a far greater chance of achieving them.

Finish these sentences:

I'm reading this book because I want to _____ .

My "why" is _____ .

Hopefully, you took some time to answer. Knowing what you want is the first step to designing a business that will bring you real wealth.

WHAT DOES REAL WEALTH MEAN TO YOU?
What is your definition of "real wealth"? For some people, it's a big house, a hefty bank account, a fancy car, or lots of zeros and commas on their net worth statement. Those can be nice—but they are only indicators of *monetary* wealth.

There are other types of wealth.

We believe that real wealth is the ability to live life on your own terms. It's about having the money and the freedom to do what you want, when you want, with the people you want to be with, and—most importantly—to enjoy each moment.

Money alone is not real wealth; it's just a tool to design your life in a way that makes you feel alive and fulfilled.

That's why we focus on a more complete and holistic perspective on wealth—one that includes financial freedom, a sense of purpose, your legacy, giving back, and living your best life. Ultimately, this type of wealth means you're in control of your finances and your life choices. As Henry David Thoreau put it: "Wealth is the ability to fully experience life."

Close your eyes and think about your version of wealth for a few minutes.

Then finish this sentence:

To me, real wealth means _____ .

WHAT ARE YOUR PERSONAL VALUES?

Take a few minutes now to answer these questions.

1. Think about the times in your life when you felt like things were really working for you—when you felt fulfilled. Describe these times in detail. What made them fulfilling?
2. Think about the times in your life when you felt off—when you felt frustrated or unfulfilled or angry. Describe these times in detail. What made them so unfulfilling?

Sometimes we have an easier time knowing what we *don't* want than what we *do* want, so when you're looking at the list of the upsetting and frustrating times, flip them. For example, if you really get angry when you are late on a payment, the opposite of that would be "financially organized." If you are frustrated when you don't have time to work out or eat well, the opposite might be "healthy living."

Now, from these exercises, you should be able to pull a list of your personal values. If you've felt fulfilled in the past by spending quality time with your kids, a personal value would be spending time with family. List as many of your personal values from these exercises as you can.

Next, go through that list and move to the top the ones that you couldn't live without. All the values are important, but your *driving values* are the ones you would keep on the list if you were only allowed to have five or six of them.

Your personal values will usually carry over to your business core values, as your business is often a reflection of you. And once you know your personal vision, you will be able to answer this key question: How can your *business* help you live your *personal* values to the fullest?

Building Wealth and Giving Back: One Man's Real Estate Mission to End Veteran Homelessness

In Southern California for a business meeting, Eric Upchurch was sitting in bumper-to-bumper traffic on the 405 freeway when he looked at the thousands of cars around him and thought, *All of us are working so hard to get to meetings or appointments that probably won't be remembered in any significant way or make that much of an impact in the end.*

He started to imagine what he would want his kids to say about him in his eulogy, and wondered what he could do with his time that *would* be remembered.

It's not that uncommon to see homeless encampments while driving around Los Angeles. Eric wondered how many of those homeless people were veterans. Since there are currently about 33,000 homeless veterans,[6] Eric thought, *Probably a lot.*

That's the moment everything changed.

What if I could end veteran homelessness? he thought.

Eric's passion to help veterans was not new. An Army Special Operations veteran, he completed five combat deployments and managed a squad of twenty-seven. He always encouraged his team to further their education, as he knew the power of it: He had a master's degree in aeronautical science, which had brought him much success in life. When Eric later became a real estate investor, he wanted to teach veterans the secrets of passive income through real estate. He cofounded Active Duty Passive Income, an educational resource for veterans with more than 80,000 members worldwide.

But solving veteran homelessness? That was a mission he wasn't sure how to tackle, and certainly not by himself. After some inquiries, he found out about Veterans Community Project, a nonprofit established in Kansas City (where he was living). Eric immediately signed up to be chair of their national fundraising program. So far, he has raised half a million dollars, which has provided a lot of homes for veterans. While that's nowhere near what's needed, Eric says it's a solvable problem with what he believes has a $250 million price tag.

"Some people might think it's too hard to raise that much money. But I say, 'No. That's not hard. What's hard is serving your country and then living under a bridge. That's hard.'"

With a purpose to serve, educate, and inspire veterans, and a mission to end veteran homelessness this decade, Eric stands out

---

6   "The State of Veteran Homelessness," U.S. Department of Veterans Affairs, 2022, https://www.va.gov/HOMELESS/State-of-Veteran-Homelessness-2022.pdf

in the crowded space of real estate. Wealthy veterans have come to him to support the cause and invest in his real estate projects. As his impact project grows, so does his business.

Eric says, "If you are looking for your purpose and mission, start to notice what lights you up, and what chokes you up. Driving through Southern California and passing homeless encampments that I knew were full of veterans certainly choked me up. We can't change it overnight, but house by house, we can make a dent. Just do one good thing today and do it again tomorrow. You will see a difference."

DEFINE YOUR PERSONAL VISION (BEFORE DEFINING YOUR COMPANY VISION)

Creating a clear and motivating personal vision will help you build a compelling vision for your company. Having a clear target of where you want to go (the top of the mountain) and then finding a way to enjoy yourself on the journey to the peak is the key.

Our friend Tarl Yarber has flipped more than 650 homes in his career. He worked hard for many years to make that happen, and he felt like there was no time to enjoy life with his family and friends. Before he started his business, he traveled, snowboarded, rock climbed, and had other adventures, but with all the hours he was working, he had to put most of those activities on hold. Then his mentor suggested "build your business around your life rather than building your life around your business."

Isn't that great? What does that mean to you? To us, it means if you put most of your focus on your business, you can go broke in life.

Early on, we made the mistake of defining the company vision before our personal visions. For many years, we've been teaching others how to build passive income through cash-flowing real estate in growth markets. Our business has been very successful, and we've helped thousands of people live their dreams thanks to their real estate portfolios. However, one day we realized that we hadn't been clear on our own real estate goals. We had not taken the time to figure out how much of our business income would go toward our personal vision versus back into the company. It's a common trap to reinvest everything in the business while falling short on personal goals. That's why our personal goals need to be clear, spelled out, and in front of us every day.

Once we got clear on our personal financial vision, we were able to get back on track. But had we not, we would be decades older and wondering where the time went and why we weren't in the same position as our clients. It's kind of like the contractor who never finishes remodeling his own home!

Understanding your personal vision is a game changer. But how do you get clear on that vision?

Here are a few questions for you. Close your eyes after reading each of these and see what comes up for you. Then open your eyes and write it down.

- When you imagine yourself in ten years, what do you look like? What are you doing?
- Twenty years from now, if everything turned out just right for you, what would life look like? In all areas: family, friends, finances, fitness, whatever. This is not a calculated and planned vision; that's a plan. This is the time to think optimistically about what you'd really want if life worked out exactly how you wanted it to.
- Who are you in twenty years? What value are you bringing to the world? What difference are you making? When people speak about you, what are they saying?
- Who do you see in your future? What family, friends, business associates, employees, or anyone else might play a significant role in your amazing future life?
- What would you do with your life if you had all the money you needed to cover your living expenses and basic needs, along with all the money you needed for the things you *want* to do?

Your Mindset Is the Foundation of Your Future Self

Dan Coleman, our business coach whom we mentioned in Chapter 1, has seen that having the right mindset is a critical key to success.

"Nothing happens without the proper mindset," he says. "Part of the mindset piece is: Know yourself. Like, know yourself outside of journaling. Leverage frameworks like Kolbe or DISC [which we address in Chapter 8] or the Six Types of Working Genius. Really know yourself, what your weaknesses and strengths are, what lights you up and what sucks energy out of you.

"It's about future-self management. Who is your future self? Because that will dictate your mindset and what you're doing today. Your activities that you actually spend time on today will be dictated not by your past, not by incremental growth, but by who you want to be in three to five years. You could literally 10x everything in your life in three years if you wanted to."

HAVE A CLEAR DESTINATION

A RealWealth client came to us years ago with a very clear personal vision: He wanted to be a full-time artist. He wanted to spend his days painting, sculpting, and creating, and not have to worry about money. I (Kathy) asked him how much money he would need to be able to cover his basic expenses. He replied, "$3,000 per month. I live simply. I just want an abundance of free time."

Earning $3,000 passively would require about $360,000 invested at a 10 percent return. This was a goal I knew he could achieve. We put together a plan, and he was able to live his dream within eighteen months. Without having to worry about making money, he was able to pour himself fully into his art. Not surprisingly, he became a rather successful artist.

When we have a clear vision, we are more willing to put in the extra time and effort it takes to get there. Without a clear destination, the business is our destination.

IT STARTS WITH YOU

When you decided to become a full-time entrepreneur, you may have decided that you would not depend on anyone but yourself for your own financial success. That's a big commitment. The more clarity you have about why you made that decision and what success looks like in your future, the more it will help you develop a plan for your business that aligns your future team, better serves your customers or clients, and helps you design your business around your life.

Growing your business based on your personal vision is a powerful way to become a better version of yourself. Why? Because you will always be learning and expanding, and never complacent with time or your life. You will continue to move toward your vision, which will bring you more fulfillment, energy, and happiness. And who doesn't want that?

TAKEAWAYS

Getting clear on your personal "why," your values, your definition of real wealth, and your personal vision will help you:

▶ Better recognize the opportunities, people, and resources that might help you move toward your vision.
▶ Define how you want your business to support your vision.
▶ Find guidance when things get tough and you feel like you're stuck in the muck, since knowing your personal vision will act as your "neon sign" on the other side of the swamp.
▶ Feel more fulfilled and help you clarify the core values of your business.

PART II
WHAT'S YOUR BUSINESS ABOUT?

CHAPTER 3
YOUR BUSINESS BLUEPRINT: DESIGNING YOUR STRATEGIC PLAN

Effort and courage are not enough without purpose and direction.

—PRESIDENT JOHN F. KENNEDY

In Chapter 2, we emphasized the importance of being clear about your personal "why," your core values, and your personal vision. Knowing what personally drives you is what will help you shape the strategic plan for your business, designing it in a way that honors your personal goals while also defining the aspirations of your business. Creating a blueprint for your company will keep you focused on its strategic direction (the purpose, mission, and vision) and its guiding principles (the values and beliefs).

We'll call this your "business blueprint," and it's what we'll delve into in this chapter.

Note: As we mentioned in the introduction, please keep in mind that the information in this book is designed for businesses that are already established and ready to scale, not for those in the early stages or just launching.

If you're wanting to scale smart, you need to be clear in your business blueprint about your target customers and what they need, and know what differentiates your business. The key elements of your blueprint are your purpose, mission, and vision—what we call PMV. Each of these plays a crucial role when you're laying the groundwork for intelligent business growth.

You will also need to assemble a fantastic team to keep your company on the right track. Later in this chapter, we'll dive into the foundational steps for discovering, retaining, and motivating a team around your crystal clear PMV.

PURPOSE: THE "WHY"

Your business purpose is basically your big business "why." Your personal "why" is usually about you: what you want in your life, what is important to you, and how you want to live. Your business "why" is more about the objective for which your company exists, which guides your decisions and actions. It typically goes beyond making a profit and often focuses on the broader societal or customer needs that your business intends to solve.

Ultimately, your business purpose serves as a guiding star that helps shape your company's mission and vision. It gives direction and meaning to your organization's activities. Plus, it's a powerful tool for building your brand identity, gaining employee and customer loyalty, and earning trust from stakeholders. Your business purpose doesn't change. It's not a time-bound goal. It's about what you do and who you do it for. It's why your company exists.

Identifying Your "Why" for Real Estate

Lisa Song Sutton was the first Miss Nevada of Asian descent. She made many friendships during her time in the spotlight, which served her well when she later became a real estate agent. Lisa succeeded in closing one of the largest transactions in Las Vegas at the time, only to find out that some of her colleagues had tried to secretly steal her high-net-worth clients.

This is when she discovered a new purpose: starting her own brokerage—one that would be rooted in trust, collaboration, and honesty rather than fierce competition and deceit. Today, she owns an all-female team of real estate agents. Her mission is to ensure that all her team members not only own their primary residences but are also able to acquire investment properties. She does this through high-level education and mentorship, ensuring that her employees "walk the talk" and can accomplish what they are helping others accomplish.

For Lisa, having a clear purpose, mission, and vision has attracted people with similar values. She now has co-CEOs who run the brokerage full time, which has freed her up for another passion: supporting veteran-owned start-ups. She launched The Veteran Fund, which invests in high-growth military technology start-ups founded by veterans. Her vision stems from her father's military service and passion to defend his country. Lisa is no stranger to the power of purpose and as such has attracted three general partners to help run the fund.

MISSION: THE BIG GOAL

While your purpose is the broad objective for which your company exists, your business mission is a short and sweet statement that sets the intention. It's the big, audacious goal you aim to achieve within a set time frame; a specific milestone that you can measure progress toward.

The time frame for a mission is usually three to five years, but could be up to ten years out, depending on how big the mission is. When you reach your mission, you will need to set a new mission. For example, if your business purpose is to explore space, your mission might be reaching the moon by a specific date. Once you've landed on the moon, you set your sights on the next cosmic stop, maybe Mars. That becomes your new mission.

Your mission keeps you on track while you continue your journey in line with your business purpose.

VISION: THE SNAPSHOT OF THE FUTURE

Finally, your business vision is just that: a vision of what you see for your company in the future if everything were to turn out just right. It describes what you want the journey to look like as you continue moving toward your mission, ever guided by your purpose.

Cameron Herold, author of *Vivid Vision: A Remarkable Tool for Aligning Your Business Around a Shared Vision of the Future,* describes business vision—or, as he calls it, Vivid Vision—as "a three-dimensional world that you can step into and explore. It's a world you can share with your team to create true alignment and amazing results. It's a true road map that helps your team see where to go."

We love that explanation of a vision, and we love visioning! There is no "figuring out how to get there" in the visioning process. It's just about imagining how you see your company looking and feeling if everything were to go according to plan, without getting bogged down by details, data, and numbers. Vision is not about "How will we do this?" It's about "How does it look and feel as we do this?"

Here is a graphic of our company's purpose, mission, and values.

REALWEALTH®

Our Purpose
We help people create *real* wealth.
"Having the money and the freedom to live life on your own terms."

Our Mission
To help our members acquire over $3.5 billion in real estate assets by the year 2030.

Our Core Values
we are ATOMIC!

Accountability
We do what we say we will do
We take ownership and responsibility
We hold each other accountable

Transparency
We practice open and honest communication
We share our thoughts and feelings with each other
We check our egos at the door and we're willing to be vulnerable

Optimism
We start with trust and then verify
We look for the best in others and their dreams, ideas, and goals.
We see challenges as adventures and face them with creativity and positivity

Mastery
We understand that as we get better, everything around us gets better
We strive for continuous improvement—personal, professional, intellectual, & financial
We follow the path of patient, dedicated effort, without attachment to immediate results

Integrity
We walk the talk
We do the right thing
We understand that honesty is always the best policy

Connection
We connect people
We care and we share
We are like family and we're better together

Our Guiding Principles
- We are entrepreneurial;
- We value freedom and balance;
- We discover and apply our unique abilities;
- We love to have fun, be silly, and work playfully;
- We respect each other, count on each other, and love one another;
- We care for our society, our partners, our investors, our customers, and our employees.

*Atomic (ə'tämik / adjective)

1 A single irreducible unit or component in a larger system.
2 Relating to, denoting, or using the energy released in nuclear fusion
(origin: late 17th century: from modern Latin atomicus, 'indivisible')

WHY A BUSINESS BLUEPRINT IS NECESSARY FOR SMART SCALING

Creating a business blueprint might seem like an unnecessary chore, but it's key to successfully running and scaling your business. Let's look at all the benefits of having a purpose, mission, vision, and values.

BUSINESS PURPOSE: WHAT ENERGIZES YOU AND YOUR TEAM

Having a real passion for your business is an absolute must for keeping it going strong in the long run. When you're truly fired up about your business and it aligns with your core values, it's like a spark that ignites not just you, but your whole team.

For us, it all stemmed from a simple personal "why": the desire to live life on our terms. We wanted financial freedom and time freedom, living abundantly instead of worrying about scarcity. We'd been through those stressful times when bills piled up, taxes loomed, and the mortgage weighed heavy. When money stress crept in, it was tough to be the cool, loving, and grounded folks we aimed to be. Financial worries made it hard to keep that joyful, positive energy flowing. Sound familiar?

We took our personal "why" and used it to create our business purpose: helping other people create real wealth. To us, this means having both the money and freedom to live life on your own terms. It's about erasing those money worries so you can be a better parent, a better partner, and a better human being.

We share that purpose with every one of our employees. When we interview someone to work for our company, we tell them our purpose and ask them questions about their purpose and what's important to them. We also share our core values and ask them to explain an event in their life where one of those core values was being honored, or not honored, and how it made them feel. This helps us—and them—get a feel for if they're a good fit for our company.

Now, let's talk about money. Money's awesome, no doubt about it, and it's a blast to make lots of it. But here's the kicker—when your business is built on purpose, it feels fantastic too, and it can even boost your revenue.

Economists have always argued that money can't buy happiness, but compensation is still a major factor for us when it comes to work. According to the Adecco Group, 45 percent of people surveyed would consider a new job if they could get a better salary.[7] But research has shown that, regardless of income level, what really keeps us satisfied at work isn't just the paycheck—it's the culture, the values, and the overall "vibe" of the company.[8]

At RealWealth, our business "why" is helping people create real wealth through carefully selected income-generating properties in growth markets, but we also have a business "how": to be a conscious capitalism company or, simply put, a conscious company. (Thanks to John Mackey, the cofounder of Whole Foods, for promoting these principles.) Conscious capitalism means businesses operate ethically while pursuing profits and considering all stakeholders—not just management and shareholders, but society, partners, investors, customers, and employees too.

Having a crystal clear business purpose has been a game changer for us and the other companies we've featured in this book. When you're clear about your purpose and your team gets behind it, there's an incredible energy that flows through your organization, from team to team and person to person. That energy attracts customers who resonate with your purpose, who think, *I want to be part of this.*

BUSINESS MISSION: WHAT KEEPS EVERYONE MOVING IN THE RIGHT DIRECTION

Your mission for the company serves as a guiding intention over a clearly defined amount of time. It communicates a fundamental reason for your business to be here. A well-crafted mission is typically clear, concise, inspirational, and measurable. Its main purpose is to put a stake in the ground that says, "This is what we are focused on for the next X years. This is what we will rally around. This is what we will achieve for the greater good. We are all in!"

A well-crafted mission typically includes the following elements:

- **Purpose:** Your mission is based on the core reason for your company's existence.
- **Values:** Your mission will often uphold your company's core values and guiding principles. These help guide your company's behavior,

---

7   "The Future of Work Beyond the Pandemic: Takeaways from our Global Workforce of the Future Report," The Adecco Group, September 27, 2022, https://www. adeccogroup.com/future-of-work/latest-insights/the-future-of-work-beyond-the-pandemic#.

8   Caroline Styr, "5 Things that Make workers Stay at Their Jobs (Hint: It's Not Salary)," World Economic Forum, December 15, 2022, https://www.weforum.org/agenda/2022/12/5-things-that-make-workers-stay-at-their-jobs-not-salary/.

decision-making, and interactions with customers, employees, and your community. Your values help create the "vibe" of your company.

The mission helps your employees better fulfill your company's purpose and align their efforts with its objectives. Additionally, it will often resonate with customers and investors, conveying your company's commitment to delivering value.

Mission vs. Goals

Your mission is like a big, shared, compelling goal—but it's also different. The mission typically provides a guiding framework for your company's activities and decisions for a specific period. It helps set the tone and direction for your organization.

On the other hand, goals in a business context are specific, measurable, and time-bound objectives that your company aims to achieve. Goals are more specific than a mission. They represent the desired outcomes or achievements a company is working toward in the short term. Goals can be set in various areas, such as sales, profitability, market share, product development, or customer satisfaction.

Back in 2014, we decided to sit down and create a mission for our business, RealWealth. What we came up with was simple: to assist 50,000 people in improving their financial intelligence and working toward that sweet real-wealth dream of living life on their own terms.

We brainstormed different ways we could help our members reach that goal. Maybe it would be through an educational blog post, or perhaps an eye-opening webinar would do the trick. Some folks would join us at live events and learn from our awesome speakers, while others would take the plunge and invest in properties through us, getting closer to financial freedom. No matter how they got there, every person who joined RealWealth would be a win in our book.

We set an ambitious target of getting 50,000 members by the end of 2020. To be honest, when we first set it, we had no clue how we'd attract all those people. But guess what? When December 31, 2020, rolled around, we had a whopping 51,234 members! It felt incredible to not just meet but surpass our goal, and we celebrated this achievement with our entire team.

But here's the thing—we didn't want to rest on our laurels. We realized that having a clear mission was like a secret sauce that inspired our entire team. After basking in the glory of our 2020 success, our team came up with a new idea: They suggested we find a fresh way to track our progress in living our business purpose, and that's when we decided to create something we call the RealWealth Assessment—which can be found at www. RealWealth.com/assessment. It's a twenty-question quiz that helps people measure how they're feeling about their finances and money management.

We developed the assessment to help people measure, manage, and track their progress over time in the areas of life that bring them real wealth and fulfillment. If someone has adopted a straightforward-yet-disciplined approach to setting themselves up for financial freedom and living what they define as their "best life," they would probably get a score between 50 and 70. The typical score for most people who take the assessment for the first time is around 60. Scores over 80 are uncommon. And anything above 90? That's like spotting a unicorn.

But here's the cool part: After putting plans in place and sticking to them for a year, most folks will find themselves above 70, and after two years, it's not unusual to hit 80.

We created a mission for our business: Get 500 of our members to 80 or better on the assessment in three years. Instead of simply acquiring new members every month, we were able to quantify the benefit they were receiving by becoming a member.

Today we have a new mission: help our members acquire over $3.5 billion in real estate assets by 2030. We believe real estate is the greatest wealth builder of all, and if we can help families grow their real estate portfolios, they can experience more real wealth from passive income and equity growth.

BUSINESS VISION: THE CAPTIVATING PICTURE OF THE FUTURE

While your personal vision might be similar to that of your business, it's crucial to recognize that your business needs its own vision. Your company's vision should resonate with the dreams and needs of your clients, employees, and community. If you don't have a company vision, your personal vision might take over, which can be a snooze fest for both your clients and employees.

When things get tough—as they always do—and your team feels like they're trudging through the mud while striving to perform better, serve better, and produce a superior product or service, having a compelling business vision that everyone has bought into will keep your team moving forward. That's a reason involving your key team members in shaping your business vision is so valuable.

You don't want to create just any old vision. Simply aiming to "hit $5 million in revenue," "double our profits," or "own this many units" won't inspire everyone on your team. It might only fire up a few, especially if their pay is directly tied to those goals. Even then, that motivation might fizzle out quickly.

Humans aren't solely motivated by money, despite what you might see on social media or reality TV or hear from self-proclaimed gurus. We all know that money is just a tool to meet our needs. When current market conditions or challenging customers are hindering your team's progress, or they're feeling overwhelmed by all the systems, processes, and checklists they need to follow, a team that is aligned with the business vision can sharpen focus on what really matters and become super committed and truly unstoppable.

Various surveys and studies consistently reveal the same thing: Finding purpose and meaning in one's work has a significant impact on job satisfaction and overall well-being. Employees who believe their work aligns with their personal values and makes a meaningful impact on society tend to be more engaged and satisfied in their roles.

According to Andrew Chamberlain, PhD, the chief economist at Glassdoor, "Across all income levels, the top predictor of workplace satisfaction is not pay: It is the culture and the values of the company, followed closely by the quality of senior leadership and the career opportunities at the company."[9] Chamberlain and his research partner, data scientist Patrick Wong, reached this conclusion by surveying more than 615,000 Glassdoor users who had reported their pay and reviewed their employer since 2014.

We're not saying that compensation doesn't matter. Salary is undoubtedly essential for many employees, especially when it comes to meeting financial needs, supporting families, and achieving financial security. However, a good paycheck alone won't keep your employees happy or fulfilled if your company lacks a strong culture, a meaningful purpose, and excellent leadership.

As you build your team, think about how to motivate and inspire them to embody your culture and excel in their roles. We'll show you

---

9 Andrew Chamberlain, "What Matters More to Your Workforce than Money," *Harvard Business Review,* January 17, 2017, https://hbr.org/2017/01/what-matters-more-to-your-workforce-than-money.

how you can do this in later chapters of this book. Share your compelling vision, and together, you'll be an unstoppable force as you scale your business.

HOW TO IDENTIFY YOUR COMPANY'S CORE VALUES

Using the feedback from the visioning exercises, you will be able to identify some of the core values that are important to your entire organization. These values should reflect what your company stands for and guide its future actions. As we mentioned earlier in this book, it can help to come up with your own ideas for the company values based on your own values. Use these as a starting point and then ask your team for their input.

When Rich has coached other companies on building out their core values, he always starts with the founder's values and then asks the leadership team or all employees (if they are part of the meeting) for their thoughts on the values that are important to the founders. Those core values usually last, sometimes with a slight modification, and sometimes with another couple of values added if they are shared by most of the people in the room.

WHY CORE VALUES HELP STRENGTHEN YOUR COMPANY CULTURE

Values are like your go-to guide: They help everyone in your company know how to act and make choices. It's like having a secret code that keeps your team on the same wavelength, boosting the company vibe to be stronger and making people feel more connected. Plus, when a company's values match what everyone's aiming for, it feels like everyone is rowing a boat together in the same direction. This shared journey makes work way more meaningful and keeps everybody chasing the same dreams.

Also, strong values are a people magnet. They pull in people who get what the company is all about and stick around because they genuinely love it. When you're working with people who share your values, everyone's happier and more on their A game. When a company is all about honesty and being open, it leads to a trusted, transparent workplace. This means top-notch teamwork, and the company is just a cooler place to work. Plus, if a company digs creativity and learning, it's way more likely to stay current and flexible. Keeping up with the times and being ready to innovate is a big deal, especially when things change fast.

A strong set of values is like having a sturdy foundation: It helps your company stay solid over time, ready to tackle anything that comes its way.

Core Values and Company Culture

Our friend Tarl Yarber, whom we mentioned in Chapter 2, is the founder of Fixated Real Estate and Fixated Events. He and his team specialize in real estate systems for success and are considered experts in the investment industry. Tarl is passionate about helping others scale their businesses to the next level, and he and his team produce some of the largest real estate and business growth conferences throughout the United States. Since 2011, Tarl has also completed more than 650 single-family fix-and-flips and has learned some important lessons about hiring, managing, and leading people. Here's what he says about company culture and core values:

"No one has ever wished they fired someone slower ... we all wish we fired them sooner. The wrong person on the team can create massive toxicity throughout the entire organization if not checked. Be very mindful of the company core values and culture. Skill is not the most important factor on a team. Skill can be trained. However, character, personality, loyalty, work ethic, motivation, integrity, and more cannot be trained.

"The biggest setbacks in my business have all come from hiring someone who did not fit the core values and culture of our companies, and then not firing them soon enough. I watch this like a hawk today, and my team watches it even closer. The culture demands this."

OUR CORE VALUES: HOW WE BECAME ATOMIC

It took us years to finalize our company's core values. When we first identified them, we had a list of nine. It was a good start, but we had so many that it was difficult to remember them all. We even did a contest one year at our annual retreat where whoever could name our nine core values would get $20 on the spot. Only one person was able to do it; that was a clear sign we needed to revisit our core values and narrow down the list.

We had a hard time eliminating any of the values because they all had great meaning to us. Instead, we decided to blend two or three values into one. We ended up with a list of six values that were all very important to everyone on our team. As we wrote them on the whiteboard, one of our employees said, "Hey, if we arrange these in a different way, it will spell the word ATOMIC!" It was such a great idea, because having an acronym has made our core values easy to remember. Now, when we randomly ask someone on our team what our core values are, they can rattle them off without a problem.

These are our ATOMIC core values:

Accountability: We do what we say we will do. We take ownership and responsibility.
Transparency: We practice open and honest communication.
Optimism: We see challenges as adventures and face them with creativity.
Mastery: We strive for continuous improvement—personally and professionally.
Integrity: We walk the talk, and we do the right thing.
Connection: We connect people. We care and we share. We're better together.

The word "atomic" is defined as a "single irreducible unit or compound in a larger system."[10] So our single values all come together to create a larger system with a lot of power!

A Real Example of PMV

When I (Kathy) first started RealWealth, I desperately wanted to understand passive income, so I could live my personal vision. It's fine to have your personal and business visions overlap when you're a one-person show. But as you grow and hire more people, your staff won't stick around if they realize they're just there to help you achieve your personal dreams.

When I asked Rich to shift from being my "Chief Support Guy" to being my full-time business partner, we had three employees: a bookkeeper, a salesperson, and an event planner. Our company was growing quickly at that point because it was during the Great Recession, when millions of homes had gone into foreclosure. Our office was filled with people who wanted us to help them buy discounted properties. We needed to hire a lot more people to keep up with demand.

Amid the chaos, Rich organized a day for the entire staff to come together and talk about the company's purpose, mission,

---

10 *The Oxford Pocket Dictionary of Current English*, Encyclopedia.com, s.v. "Atomic," https://www.encyclopedia.com/science-and-technology/physics/physics/atomic#atomic.

and vision. The phones were ringing off the hook, and people were knocking on our doors, but Rich put up a sign saying that we were having a company meeting and that we'd be closed for the day. I was a little irritated because we had a lot of work to do and no time to discuss "fluffy" things like visions and values. But he insisted.

Rich started by affirming that our company's purpose was all about helping people build wealth through real estate investing so that they could experience financial freedom and live life the way they wanted to. Everyone was on board with that.

Then, he asked each person to imagine where our company would be in a decade. Here are some of their responses.

- Customers who are retired in ten years as a result of what they purchase today
- Charities like Habitat for Humanity have benefited enormously from our company
- Parents are better parents because their financial stress is removed
- Children are happier because their families have more quality time together
- Our members are financially savvy because we've educated them so well over the years that they know how to make great financial decisions

That day, we crafted our company vision, which included bits and pieces of everyone's ideas about the future.

Rich then explained that our next step was to create a clear mission for the next five years—a clear intention we'd all work toward.

He asked us how we could honor our purpose and make significant progress toward the ten-year vision we'd just discussed. We filled up massive posters on our office walls with ideas written on sticky notes. Then, on a fresh page, he wrote "By 2020, RealWealth will have helped over 50,000 people create real wealth by raising their financial intelligence, improving their wealth mindset, and helping them invest for their futures. In addition, we will donate over $1 million to several amazing charities that make a huge difference in people's lives."

Our company got fired up! There was a newfound inspiration and a deeper reason to show up for work every day. We knew we were going to change lives and help people. We all felt aligned and inspired. We weren't just selling real estate; we were selling a lifestyle that real estate supported. We proudly displayed our mission on our website, and our customers resonated with it, leading to packed events and skyrocketing sales.

HOW TO CREATE YOUR PURPOSE, MISSION, AND VISION

Now that you've learned how important PMV is, it's time to write one for your business. Grab a pen and paper (or use your computer or phone), and allow your imagination to soar!

YOUR BUSINESS PURPOSE

Reflect on your personal "why" from Chapter 2 and ask yourself:

- How can my business purpose support what matters most to me?
- What about my personal purpose can I bring to my company and my team that will fire up *everyone* to make a difference in the world?

Now, take a moment and think about the driving force of your company. What problem is your product or service solving? What need is it filling? What is the difference it's making in the world? How will the world be better because of what you provide?

You may already have a clear idea of your company's purpose. If you don't, then fill out these sentences:

"We help _____ get _____."

"We solve _____ so that _____ can
_____."

"We support _____ in getting _____."

YOUR BUSINESS MISSION

Now it's time to shoot for the moon and put your intention and some numbers down on paper. What is the big goal you and your team want to accomplish in the next three to five years that will move your company toward your purpose?

Here are some questions to help you:

- How many people will you help?
- How many products will you sell?
- How much will you donate?
- What measurable outcome will your business achieve?

YOUR BUSINESS VISION (TEN YEARS)

One of the things that most Olympic gold medalists have in common is their ability to repeatedly visualize the perfect outcome of their performance. As a competitive ice skater, I (Kathy) was trained to do the same—close my eyes before every competition and see myself successfully performing every single move of my routine. Sometimes I couldn't see it and would have to work through those blocks in my mind before I hit the ice (both figuratively and literally!). If your subconscious can't envision it, it generally won't happen in reality. So much of our work needs to happen in our minds first. That really is the first step. You can use these same powerful methods for your business.

Let's do this. Take a moment to dream. Put your feet on the ground, uncrossed, hands in your lap, eyes closed. Take three slow, deep breaths.

You are about to take a mental journey. When you're ready, imagine that you are transported into the future ten years from now. Where do you land? What is around you? What is Future You doing? Who are you doing it with?

Imagine that you are following your future self around, seeing how you start your workday, where you are going, what you are doing.

Imagine that you check in on the business. How many employees does it have? What are they doing? How has your product or service improved? How does it stand out from the competition?

Imagine that you check in on some customers. What are they saying about your company? Are they raving about you? If any negative thoughts come in, notice them and then shift your thoughts to this visit being a positive experience.

Imagine visiting your bookkeeper. What is the company's annual revenue? What kind of profit is the company experiencing?

Perhaps you observe each employee and overhear what they are saying. How have their lives changed from this company? What are they raving about?

Toward the end of the day, imagine that you are all dressed up for a celebration. It's a company party. What are you celebrating? Where is it? How did you get there? Who is with you? Who are you honoring? Who is honoring you?

Now come back to the present day and open your eyes. Write down everything you envisioned.

You can also do this exercise with your team and share the various visions on a whiteboard to help create your company's ten-year vision.

(We will discuss this more in Chapter 4.) Remember, you don't need to know exactly how you will get there; you and your team just need to be excited about the vision you create.

Choose a future date for your business vision.
3 years, 5 years, or 10 years.
Write down the actual month, day, and year for this vision.

Have your team close their eyes and then imagine moving into the future to that date.

Remind everyone what your business purpose is by saying something like: "Our company X years in the future has continued to follow our purpose of _____."

Question #1
Imagine that you're at a special annual event for our company. Who is there? Where is the event being held?

Question #2
Now imagine that someone gets up to share some big news about the company. What do they share?

Question #3
Now imagine that there are several of your company's clients or customers in attendance. What do they say about how the company has helped them?

Question #4
Now imagine that the company has grown and matured. What has changed? What is new?

Question #5
Now imagine that there is a number that appears on a screen. This number represents something significant. What is that number?

KEEP YOUR PMV IN FRONT OF YOU

The key to keeping PMV alive is focusing on it. This is why you often see companies post their purpose, mission, and vision in large print on their walls. You want to have your PMV in front of you as much as possible. Rich even has our PMV printed out in a binder, along with his personal and professional goals, and he reviews them every morning.

When our team is trying to solve problems, they go to our PMV for insight. When they come up with a new idea, they first run it through the PMV to make sure it aligns. At our monthly all-company updates, quarterly retreats, and annual planning sessions, we revisit our purpose, mission, and vision together.

HOW TO PUT YOUR VISION AND VALUES INTO ACTION

Your company culture is your vision and values in action. In the next chapter, we will cover how to make the most of your company's vision and its core values, so you can create and maintain an amazing culture.

TAKEAWAYS

PURPOSE

▶ Your business purpose is essentially your business "why." It's a statement that defines the core reason for your company's existence.

▶ Your company's purpose serves as a guiding star that helps shape your mission, vision, decisions, goals, and actions.

▶ Having a real passion for your business is an absolute must for keeping it going strong in the long run.

MISSION

▶ Your mission is an intention for your company set over a clearly defined amount of time, usually three to five years, possibly up to ten.

▶ A well-crafted mission is clear, concise, inspirational, and measurable. It communicates the fundamental reason for your business to exist.

▶ It will inspire your employees, your customers, your investors, and anyone else who is attracted to that mission.

VISION

▶ Your business needs its own vision that is separate from your personal vision (even if they might be similar).

▶ Your company's vision should resonate with the dreams and needs of your clients, employees, and community— not just with you.

- ▶ A compelling vision injects mental energy, sharpens focus on what really matters, and gets everyone fired up about the business.
- ▶ A good paycheck won't keep your employees happy or fulfilled if your company lacks a strong culture, a meaningful purpose, and excellent leadership.

VALUES

- ▶ Your company's core values should reflect what your organization stands for and guide its future actions.
- ▶ Your business values are usually based on your own personal values.
- ▶ Core values unify your team members and help everyone know how to act and make choices.
- ▶ You don't want to have too many core values. Narrow the list down, and make them easy for everyone to remember.

AND REMEMBER ...

- ▶ Keep your PMV in front of you consistently and review it regularly—alone and with your team.

CHAPTER 4

CREATING A MAGNETIC COMPANY CULTURE

There's no magic formula for great company culture. The key is just to treat your staff how you would like to be treated.

—RICHARD BRANSON, FOUNDER, VIRGIN GROUP

Creating a self-managing business that not only does well but also gives you more freedom and makes a positive impact starts with building a strong company culture. Forbes explains company culture as "shared norms, values, attitudes, and practices that form the collective identity of your company."[11] This culture is vital when it comes to having a business that pretty much runs itself, freeing you up to focus on bigger goals and your unique strengths, and providing you with more personal freedom.

WHY DO YOU NEED A STRONG COMPANY CULTURE?

Employee empowerment is at the heart of this. A good culture creates a team of inspired leaders by making everyone feel responsible and like they own a part of the business. When employees embrace your company's purpose, mission, vision, and values (see Chapter 3), they're more likely to step up and make better decisions for the business. This leads to not only a team that's hardworking but also employees who take initiative, cutting down on the need for you to always keep an eye on things.

This kind of culture helps attract and keep the best people. Talented and driven employees who connect with what your company stands for are crucial for your business to run effectively. Your team of inspired leaders can handle operations, come up with new ideas, and adapt

---

11 Belle Wong, "What Is Company Culture? Definition & Development Strategies," *Forbes Advisor*, August 15, 2023, https://www.forbes.com/advisor/business/company-culture/.

without needing your constant input. Believe us—they don't want your constant input anyway. This keeps things running smoothly day-to-day and paves the way for scaling smart.

A strong culture also boosts your brand's image. Happy, empowered employees are the best promoters of your brand, and their positive customer interactions help build a loyal client base. This loyalty is great not just for steady income but also for word-of-mouth marketing, which can be super effective—and it's free!

An established company culture gives everyone a common way to deal with changes and challenges. Being able to adapt and bounce back is key in any business; group resilience is essential for long-term success.

Encouraging creativity and innovation is also important. A culture that values fresh ideas and problem-solving lets employees come up with new solutions, keeping your business ahead in its field. This boosts profits while making a positive difference in your market and society.

Operational efficiency also gets a big boost in a company with a solid culture. Employees know what their role is and what's expected of them, leading to smoother decision-making and operations. This efficiency is crucial for a business that is run by your team, making sure everything works well even when you're not there.

Finally, investing in your employees' growth and development is vital. Helping your team build their skills and careers not only creates a more skilled workforce, it also builds loyalty and a sense of community. This investment pays off when you have a team that can manage and grow your business independently, giving you more freedom and profitability. That's a double whammy!

The bottom line is that a strong company culture is essential for a self-managing business. It empowers employees, increases effectiveness, fosters innovation, and strengthens your brand, all leading to higher profits, more freedom for you, and a positive impact on your customers and the world.

With all those awesome benefits, let's look at ways to build that strong culture at *your* company.

Hire great people and give them freedom to be awesome.

—ANDREW MASON, FOUNDER, GROUPON

HOW TO CREATE YOUR COMPANY CULTURE BY BUILDING A COMPANY VISION

In Chapter 3, we discussed how to create your business purpose, mission, and vision. This was a solo endeavor, as you began to envision your business and lay a path for success. As your business begins to grow and you have more employees who contribute to your business's success, you may need to rework and develop your overall vision with the company culture in mind.

Having your whole team be part of your visioning process can mean a big improvement to company culture and loyalty. When you have a compelling future vision for your company, it helps the entire team stay aligned and move in the same direction. Here are some key steps that can help you create your company vision.

- **Gather input:** In the next section, we'll show you how you can take your team through a visualization process to create your company culture. You don't have to have a structured process for gathering your team's input—but it sure does work! You could simply ask everyone to journal their ideas or just do a simple brainstorming session. Ask them about their views on the company's current state, future direction, and values. This inclusive approach ensures that the vision resonates with your employees, as they feel their voices are heard and valued.
- **Define the vision:** Craft a clear, inspiring vision statement that encapsulates where the company is heading in three to ten years. It doesn't really matter how many years into the future the vision is. What matters is that the vision is ambitious yet achievable, and it should align with the core values. It's also important that the vision is easy to understand and communicate. You can write it in bullet-point form or in story form—whatever is going to be inspiring for the whole team and will be reviewed often.
- **Communicate the vision:** Share the vision with all your employees consistently and through different methods. This could include company meetings, newsletters, and internal communication platforms. It's important that your leadership team consistently communicates and reinforces the vision.
- **Integrate the vision into your company culture:** The vision should be more than just a statement; it should be integrated into the day-to-day operations of your company. This includes aligning business goals, decision-making, and company policies with the vision.

- **Lead by example:** Your leadership team should embody the company vision and values in their actions. When leaders model the vision, it sets a standard for all employees to follow, which strengthens your company culture.
- **Recognize and reward alignment with the vision:** Acknowledge and reward employees who demonstrate behaviors and achievements that align with your company vision and values. This reinforces the importance of the vision and encourages others to do the same.
- **Review and adapt:** Regularly review the vision to ensure it remains relevant and resonates with both the employees and the market conditions. Be open to adapting the vision as the company grows and evolves.

By involving your employees in the development of your company vision, you help ensure it becomes a living part of your company culture. You also foster a sense of ownership and loyalty among your team. This inclusive approach not only improves morale, it also aligns everyone toward a common goal, enhancing overall company performance.

FUTURE FOCUS: BRINGING YOUR TEAM ON A TEN-YEAR VISION QUEST

A couple decades ago, when I (Rich) was a business coach, I would often lead my clients through a visualization exercise where they would imagine traveling ten to twenty years into the future to meet their "future self." My clients would ask their future self questions like "What do I need to do to get to where you are?" and they would imagine what a day in the life of their future self looked like.

In the early years of our company, I led our whole team through a session imagining the future of RealWealth. During our two-day annual retreat, I kicked things off by saying, "Okay, since we are a California-based company, let's bring a little 'woo-woo' into this conference room. We are going to take a little mental journey into the future of our company. Everyone please close your laptops, put down your pens, get into a comfortable position, and close your eyes."

After everyone did some breathwork and felt grounded and centered, I had the team imagine traveling deep into space on a beam of light (I did say that we were going to bring a little "woo-woo" into the room!). Then I had us all imagine coming back to our company's annual retreat ten years in the future. I asked, "Who do you see in the room?" Then I asked everyone to imagine big posters on the wall with things written out such as how many people we've helped, how we've helped them, how much revenue we've earned, and other measurables. I also asked everyone what their role was at the company ten years in the future. Then I said, "Now imagine that a big announcement is made. There is a big surprise for everyone! What is this surprise announcement?"

After that, I asked everyone to wiggle their fingers and toes and slowly open their eyes. There was a special feeling in the room. Our team was smiling, some wiping tears from their eyes. When we discussed what each person had seen, it was exciting, heartfelt, and inspiring. Some comments included "We had helped over 100,000 people create real wealth!", "We had donated more than $10 million to charity!", "We were having our annual retreat at an all-inclusive resort on an island!", and "We all had invested in real estate and were then job-optional, but we all still worked here because we all love our jobs!"

Yeah, it was a little weird, but it was also a lot awesome. As we continued to discuss our visioning, someone said, "Now that I've seen this future, I have a whole new perspective on the future of our company and my role in that future."

As everyone shared their experience, I wrote down what each person saw for our future on the huge sticky notes I had placed on the walls in the conference room. Then I tore off a new sheet and wrote "Our Ten-Year Vision." We began to combine the similar ideas from each person into a collaborative vision that came from our whole team.

That became our ten-year vision, and we still reflect on and build from that vision today, years later, to stay aligned, connected, and inspired to make it a reality. We have made amazing progress toward that shared vision, and it has boosted our company culture and made our team feel great about where we are heading. Since everyone on our team was included in the visioning process, everyone feels like the vision is theirs.

COMPANY CULTURE IS THE CORNERSTONE

The journey to creating a thriving self-managing business that provides you with more freedom and makes a positive impact is deeply rooted in cultivating a strong company culture. This culture forms the cornerstone that supports your business to run on autopilot, freeing you to focus on what you do best and your big-picture goals.

The heart of this culture? Making sure your team members feel like they fully own their roles. When they're really into what your company is all about—its purpose, mission, vision, and values—they step up as inspired leaders and push things forward.

This kind of culture doesn't just nurture initiative and leadership; it's also a magnet for top-notch talent. It keeps your business running smoothly and sets you up for positive growth. More than just making things work better internally, a strong culture also enhances your brand image, helps you bounce back from tough times, and sparks fresh creativity and innovation. Plus, it boosts how your company runs and helps your team grow. So many benefits, right?

Next, we will show you how to create an awesome structure for your company that allows you to scale smart. Stay tuned for more game-changing tips that'll help you build a booming, thriving, healthy business!

TAKEAWAYS

▶ A strong company culture is essential for a self-managing business. It empowers employees, increases effectiveness, fosters innovation, strengthens your brand, and delivers many other benefits.

▶ Create your company vision for ten years into the future. Include your team in the visioning process.

▶ The heart of a good culture is a team that feels like they fully own their roles. When your employees are really invested in your company's purpose, mission, vision, and values, they will step up as inspired leaders.

▶ Putting time and effort into developing your team's skills pays off, resulting in a talented and dedicated crew that moves your business toward being self-sufficient and profitable.

CHAPTER 5

DESIGNING YOUR TEAM STRUCTURE

Every company has two organizational structures: The formal one is written on the charts; the other is the everyday relationship of the men and women in the organization.

—HAROLD S. GENEEN, FORMER PRESIDENT, ITT

In this chapter, we will dive into the importance of creating a clear, simple structure for your organization. What does your business structure look like today? How many people are part of your current organization? Do you have any business partners? How many employees do you have? What about independent contractors? How do you keep the communication moving throughout your company?

Creating a clear business structure will help you figure out exactly who you need to hire—full time or part time—as well as who might already be in your company but not in the right position. Having a structure will also allow you and your team to grow your business with more ease, simpler delegation, and better odds for creating more impact and profitability. All that goodness, while improving your freedom of time. Yes, you read that right. We will explain how creating structure actually creates freedom.

HIRE THE BEST PEOPLE EFFICIENTLY

When we start businesses, oftentimes we take on many different roles. This does not mean we are necessarily good at all those roles, but money might be tight, and our time is essentially "free."

As we begin to make money, we can start to put a value on our time. What is our time worth, and how is it best spent? Perhaps more importantly, what roles should we not be doing, either because someone else could do them better or because someone else could do them cheaper? As we become more successful, we tend to get busier and simply can't do all the jobs we were doing previously—even the ones that we're good at and enjoy. It's just not sustainable.

This is the time when everything changes. We transition from being a worker wearing many different hats to being a manager of other people who are trained to wear those hats. As the business generates more income, funds can be set aside to hire more help—specifically for the areas in which we are weak. And while this delegation process is the key to scaling smart, most business owners have not been trained in the skills of hiring and managing others.

The biggest mistake we made in the beginning of our business was hiring people who were affordable but not qualified. A common strategy when people start building their business is hiring family and friends who are in need of work and therefore agreeable to perform jobs for lower pay. The hope is that they will be as fired up as you are and willing to learn. Sometimes that works, but most of the time it backfires.

The best strategy to scale your company in a way that allows you to hire the best employees is to bring in people who have expertise in something you don't, even if it's part time at first. They have the knowledge and experience to train you versus you trying to train them on something you aren't that good at in the first place. You don't have to pay for a full-time COO, CMO, or CFO (which we'll talk about in the next chapter); even when funds might be tight, you can build your business with the right people.

But how do you know where to start? Which new hire will be the one that takes your company to the next level? Putting together the right team in the right order is like building a house: You wouldn't hire the roofers until you've got the foundation and framing done. The same goes with building your business. Making an organizational chart will help you figure out what roles to hire for and when. Let's look at how to create one for your business.

FIND FREEDOM WITH AN ORGANIZATIONAL CHART

Imagine your business as a puzzle that needs to be solved. Look at each of your team members as a piece of the puzzle. What is each one contributing to the puzzle?

You may realize that someone is doing multiple jobs that keep them frazzled—perhaps you're trying to fill too many empty spaces with one puzzle piece.

You may find someone isn't doing the job they're best at—maybe you're trying to fit them into the wrong space in the puzzle.

Perhaps you have empty positions that need to be filled, so certain tasks aren't getting attention or are being done by unqualified people—and therefore the puzzle can't be solved.

New business owners often make the mistake of trying to mold their current team members to be the puzzle pieces they need. It is far more effective to determine which pieces are needed and then hire accordingly. To solve the puzzle and bring order to your company, it's helpful to create an organizational chart, or "org chart" for short.

You may already have an org chart, and if so, that's great! However, if your company is not scaling the way you want it to, it may be time for a new look at your chart.

Organizational charts should be fluid. They change constantly as the company grows. Your org chart may need to be reviewed and updated quarterly, as things change when you scale your business.

An organizational chart involves putting the right pieces of the puzzle (your employees) in the right places (your roles). It's a snapshot of the structure and reporting relationships within your company. It lays out who reports to whom and how different departments and teams are connected. For small businesses, especially those looking to grow, having an org chart is key to keeping everything organized, clear, and running smoothly.

Here's how an org chart can help you, as a business owner, create more freedom of time and focus on the bigger vision for your company.

- **Clear roles:** The chart spells out who does what in your company. This makes it clear for everyone, so you don't have to keep explaining things or get bogged down in daily tasks.
- **Simpler delegation:** You can figure out who's best suited for different jobs. This means you can trust your team more and let go of some tasks, giving you more time to focus on the vision and strategy, and your unique strengths that benefit your company. With roles and responsibilities clearly defined, your team can work more smoothly without needing constant supervision.
- **Accountability:** The organizational chart also helps you hold people accountable for their work. When everyone knows what's expected of them, it's easier to measure performance and address issues without your direct involvement. That's why some companies prefer to call the org chart their "accountability chart." But the org chart is used for so much more than accountability. It allows you to see how the puzzle

pieces fit together and how you can move them around to optimize your operations for better flow, communication, and scaling.

- **Strategic growth:** As your business expands, the chart can grow with it. This flexibility allows you to adapt to changes and seize new opportunities without feeling overwhelmed. Your org chart can be a helpful and effective planning tool for your future growth. We will show you how in a moment.
- **Free time:** All these benefits add up to more free time for you. You can spend less time putting out fires and more time enjoying your life. Sounds good, right?

Just remember, creating your org chart is only the start. You'll also need good communication, training, and a way to make sure the chart is working well. And don't forget to update it as your business grows and changes. That way, you continue to optimize your operations while increasing your time freedom.

Letting Go in Order to Grow

It takes humility to let go of something you've built. A great example of this is Josh Dorkin, the founder of BiggerPockets. His big idea, passion, and commitment created a company that, for the first time ever, allowed real estate investors to communicate with each other online.

Once the company took off, he had the wisdom and foresight to see the company needed new leadership to take it to the next level. That's when he assigned the role of CEO to one of his outstanding young employees who had shown the skill set needed for scaling. Scott Trench has taken BiggerPockets to new heights, with over 3 million members sharing information to help each other grow.

The skills needed to start a business can be completely opposite of those required to scale a business. Starting requires new ideas, risk-taking, and grit, while scaling requires systems, processes, and oversight. As we mentioned earlier, the turning point for an entrepreneur is knowing how to go from being a founder to a leader. The founder must have the courage to let go of the many jobs they took on in the beginning and hand over the reins to those who can do it even better. And even if the founder was excellent at all the jobs they did, it would be impossible to do them all well when the company has grown. Therefore, a founder must become a leader of others. If that's not their skill set, someone else needs to come in to lead and manage.

In the introduction to this book, we told you about the weekend workshop for business owners and entrepreneurs that helped us think bigger and operate smarter. The facilitators of that workshop were the CEO and the COO of a 500-person CRM (customer relationship management) software company. They obviously didn't have to hold the workshop to earn more money. They were doing it because they had a passion to help small business owners succeed. The facilitators had seen firsthand how so many of their software users were going through the same challenges that they went through in their early days, so they wanted to change some lives. They sure changed our lives!

One of the simple yet powerful exercises they asked us to do was write out our current organizational chart. They then had us list all the tasks that needed to be done within the company on sticky notes, and place those with the people currently responsible for those tasks. Since we were a small company with just a few employees, everyone wore multiple hats and had many different roles and responsibilities assigned to them—it was a lot!

Once we had updated our current org chart at the workshop, they asked us to draw our chart for the business we envisioned three years in the future. They said it was simple, but they didn't say it was easy! One thing we wanted was for us (Kathy and Rich) to be less scattered and more focused, so we kept our names at the top of the org chart in CEO and COO roles. This would mean being leaders more than doers.

Creating this org chart was incredibly difficult and took us over an hour to complete. But doing that was a complete game changer for the way we scaled our business over the next three years and beyond. It's highly doubtful our business would be where it is today had we not gone through that process to understand the key people we needed to hire to free up our time to be more focused on business growth.

If you are just a small team, your names will likely be in multiple roles on the org chart as well. And while it may seem like a waste of time to draw a chart with only a few people on it, this process will help you see all the things each of you are doing and highlight where you need the most help now and in the future.

Here is the very messy chart we drew up at that workshop.

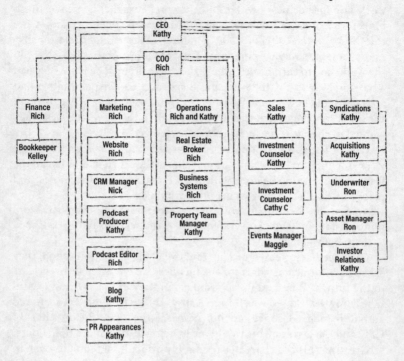

You'll see that we were involved in nearly all details of the company. You could call this a bad case of micromanaging! Rich was still spending hours editing the *Real Wealth Show* podcast, even though he was also acting as a COO. And Kathy was acting as CEO but going around her COO to work directly with nearly every employee in the company. This is what's called an "end run" in the book *Rocket Fuel,* by Gino Wickman. An end run in business means that employees can go around the managers and operations people directly to the founder, and vice versa. This disempowers the managers. As we mentioned earlier, it's very difficult for founders to let someone else care for their baby. But scaling a company requires it, because those founders will eventually become bottlenecks for the company if they don't learn to empower their employees.

Now, it's your turn.

CREATE YOUR CURRENT ORGANIZATIONAL CHART

Creating your business organizational chart is a visual way to represent the structure of your company and how its various roles and departments are organized. To get started, sketch out your current org chart, because the first step is knowing exactly where you are right now. Only then can you create the map of where you want to go.

Grab a piece of paper, sticky notes, a whiteboard, or even a napkin if that's all you can find. We recommend that you keep this more casual, so please don't create fancy slides with Google, PowerPoint, or org chart–mapping software. This should be a spontaneous, in-the-moment kind of deal, ideally in front of a few key people like your cofounders or leadership team. Keep it cozy though—no more than five or six people. When we did this exercise, it was just us two.

Here's a simple step-by-step guide to sketch it out.

1. **Start at the top:** At the top of your chart, draw a rectangle to represent the main leader or decision-maker in your company. This is typically the chief executive officer (CEO), president, or owner. Write that title inside the rectangle. Things can get complicated when there's more than one final decision-maker at the top. Who decides how things will go? Who's in control? If you have a partner and haven't determined who the final decision-maker is, this can lead to conflict. A co-CEO model can work, and we tried it for a few years, but it caused more conflict in our marriage than we were willing to have.

   Remember when we discussed how your business can support your personal vision in Chapter 2? Our personal vision was to stay happily married. Being co-CEOs threatened that, so we had to pivot. One of us had to step aside and let the other be the final decision-maker while still following our broader vision and mission.

   With a business degree and successful exits from former businesses, Rich was more suited to be a CEO than Kathy. Several years ago, he took on that role, while also being a very good listener to Kathy's needs, concerns, and desires. Plus, he is skilled at priming the other leaders in our company, who we hope will eventually run things when we are ready to retire. A good CEO should be able to fulfill the company's vision and mission by hiring and leading the talent who can get you there.

   We cannot emphasize enough the importance of having clarity on this top role and making sure it's the right person. This requires knowing the skill set of a CEO. As we mentioned in the last chapter, many business starters don't have the same skill sets as the person who grows the organization.

Starters are often risk-takers. They tend to be big-idea people. Companies don't get off the ground without them. But once a company is off the ground, it needs to focus on steady growth—not explosive growth—if you want to scale without crashing and burning later.

Kathy is a starter. Her ideas and passion are what created RealWealth in the beginning. The skill set of hiring and leading others was not her strength. Since she had already done her job of creating the business and working with the team to hone the company's purpose, mission, and vision, it was time for her to let go of the reins and let someone else lead.

Know thyself and know thy employees. And make sure the right people are in the right seats.

Once you get the lead person established, the rest will fall into place much more easily. If you are a starter and wondering where you fit on the chart if you're no longer the CEO, you may find you fit nicely on the board of directors.

2. **Add your key departments:** Once you've determined who is in the top box, it's time to fill out the support team. Next in line is typically the chief operations officer (COO). This is the person who oversees the operations of the company. Below the top position, draw a box and then a line to the CEO. This shows that the COO reports directly to the CEO. If you are just starting out and have a low budget, it might be the same person in both roles.

Next, draw rectangles to represent the major departments within your company, such as sales, marketing, operations, and finance. Connect these boxes to the COO position with lines. This means they report directly to the COO. In a smaller company, the organizational chart is typically much simpler than that of a larger corporation. Small companies often have fewer layers of management and a more streamlined structure.

Here are some of the key positions you might find near the top of the organizational chart in a small company.

- **Owner or founder:** In many small businesses, the owner or founder plays a central role in decision-making and leadership. They are often at the top of the organizational chart.

- **CEO (chief executive officer) or president:** In some small companies, the owner or founder may also serve as the CEO or president, responsible for overall management and strategic direction. In some cases, the owner/founder hires a CEO with managerial strengths they may not have.
- **COO (chief operations officer) or general manager:** Typically, this person is the second-in-command and reports directly to the CEO. The COO manages the business operations of the company by working closely with various department heads and supervisors to support the day-to-day activity of employees.
- **CFO (chief financial officer) or finance manager:** Handling the financial aspects of the company, including budgeting, accounting, and financial planning, may be the responsibility of a CFO or finance manager.
- **Head of sales or sales manager:** This person is in charge of sales strategies, customer relationships, and revenue generation.
- **Head of marketing or marketing manager:** Responsible for marketing efforts, including advertising, promotions, and brand management.
- **HR (human relations) manager:** In some cases, a small company may have an HR manager who handles hiring, employee relations, and other human resources issues. A lot of this work can also be outsourced to a professional employer organization (PEO). PEOs specialize in handling HR, payroll, and employee benefits packages.
- **Head of product/service development:** If your company creates products or services, there may be someone responsible for overseeing their development and improvement.

It's important to note that in small businesses or start-ups, one person may wear multiple hats and fulfill several of these roles. As we've mentioned, that's how it was for us a decade ago, and we're in good company.

Scott Trench, CEO of BiggerPockets, knows this is usually a necessary part of business growth. When reflecting on his own contributions to business growth, he explains, "There's a journey in business most will go through, and trying to skip the stages is dangerous. We start out on the front lines, doing the work ourselves. Then we learn to manage. Then we learn to operate and structure a business … and build an organizational structure. Embrace the journey. It's okay to start out by just being scrappy."[12]

But even if you or your employees are doing several jobs, put the boxes on the chart anyway, with the names of the people currently doing those jobs. On our first org chart, our names were in almost every department: marketing, sales, finance, product, and even tech. You won't know who to hire until you're clear on the job that is needed. The org chart will help you see this.

To figure out how to fill the org chart with the right people, you need to know what "right" means to you. For us, it means people who are great at that task and love to do it.

One of our first hires was our bookkeeper. We both traded off doing this job in the beginning and, while we were okay at it, neither of us enjoyed it. The woman we hired for bookkeeping was a skilled professional—plus, she loved doing it!

This is why it's so important to "know thyself and know thy team." The more diverse your team's abilities, the quicker you'll be able to scale.

As your company grows, you may add more specialized roles and expand the organizational structure. The structure of a small business is typically designed to be agile and efficient, with a focus on handling vital functions while keeping overhead and bureaucracy to a minimum.

3. **Position the roles within your departments:** For each department, add more boxes to represent the specific roles or positions you need within that department. For example, within sales, you might have a sales manager, with another box below that for each sales representative, and possibly another box for those employees who take care of customer support. Connect each of these roles to the department they belong to with lines.

4. **Show the reporting relationships:** Use lines with arrows to indicate the flow of who reports to whom. Typically, these lines should point from a lower-level position to the higher-level position they report to. For example, the line from sales representative to sales manager would have the arrow pointing to the manager.

---

12 This is from a conversation we had with Scott about business growth.

5. **Continue adding the details:** Keep adding more positions and roles within each department, working your way down the hierarchy. Focus on two to three levels down in the org chart—your direct reports and their direct reports and possibly their direct reports, if they have some. Include job titles and the names of the people currently in those positions. Remember, it might be *your* name in several of the boxes if your company is smaller and you currently handle a variety of roles. For now, avoid drawing any empty boxes or "to be hired" boxes.

This basic organizational chart is a simplified representation of your company's current structure. In larger or more complex organizations, you may have multiple layers and more intricate reporting relationships.

If it's a bit of a mess, that's your cue to slow down and chat it out with your group. This is a great chance to spot areas that may need some work or clarification. There can be a lot of value just from doing this part of the exercise.

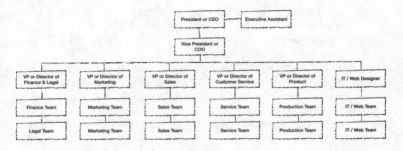

Now, take a good look at your chart and discuss it with your group. Jot down your thoughts and the feedback you get. Don't redo your chart yet. Instead, think about what seems to be working and what changes you may need to make.

Maybe someone's not quite right for their role, or their workload is off balance. Perhaps they may be better suited for another role. If they are passionate, that is more important than skill (if the skill can be learned).

Consider your direct reports. Are they diverse enough? Do they work well together, both one-on-one and as a group? Would you hire them again? Are they being paid fairly? Or does everything look just right?

Playing All the Roles at First Will Benefit You Later

Ken McElroy's expertise and success in real estate have made him a respected figure in the industry. The author of numerous excellent books on real estate investing, Ken is the founder and CEO of MC Companies, a real estate investment and property management company based in Arizona. For more than two decades, MC Companies has focused on acquiring, owning, and managing multifamily properties, with more than 300 employees, annual revenue north of $100 million, and over $1 billion in assets under management. Ken started by purchasing his first investment property while still in his early twenties. Over time, he built an impressive portfolio of properties and became an expert in leveraging debt and managing cash flow in real estate investments.

Here's what Ken has to say about performing many of the roles in your company and how it proves valuable when scaling.

"In the early years of my business, I was totally hands-on and took on most of the different roles. Over time, I had to change roles and hire new people to handle what I had been doing. I think that's a big part of business growth: You handle a lot of different roles. Then you get clear on who your next hires need to be, so you can be free to oversee the company's vision and growth. Those hires free you up to focus on leadership.

"One of the things I appreciate now is that my team knows me. I'm not out of touch. Even though our company manages over $1 billion in assets, my employees know I've walked in their shoes. They know I respect them and understand their roles. For example, I'll be in a unit with the maintenance guy, and I'm like, 'I know what you're going through. I grew up in property management. I used to paint units, replace toilets, you know, I did all that stuff.' I understand how you get tenants, the problems that come up with occupancy issues, and how to run credit and do the accounting. When I meet with my site people, who I think are the lifeblood of our whole company, I'm not bullshitting them. There's full respect from me to them and from them to me, even though I own the business.

"That's why I think it's okay in the beginning to take on lots of different roles. You learn a lot from doing that, and you better understand who to hire next and what qualities and skills to look for in that hire."

CREATE YOUR FUTURE ORGANIZATIONAL CHART

Now for a little more visioning, like you did in Chapter 2. Close your eyes and fast-forward three years. Picture how things have changed—you're older, as are your parents and kids. Imagine how your industry has changed, how the market has shifted, and how technology has advanced.

Open your eyes. You realize that your business has grown significantly. Now, create a new org chart, thinking three years ahead. You can include potential future hires this time.

Start with the CEO box—is that still you? As you fill in the chart, think about your current senior team members. Who will stick around and who won't? What would keep them engaged? Often, people stay in companies if they are respected and enjoy the workplace—and, if they are developing their skills or know-how, they can move up in the org chart.

What new positions (new boxes) will you add to your org chart? Will some of your current employees be in those positions? What will it take to help them grow? Which positions will be new hires who bring a certain level of experience?

Here's what our future org chart looked like when we first sketched it out at that business workshop; this was our plan for three years in the future. We decided to try the co-CEO model so that each of us would run one part of the business and not step on each other's toes. You can see that we created a plan for much better communication and accountability. In retrospect, what was still missing was a COO position for Kathy. She is a visionary, not an operations person, yet she was running operations!

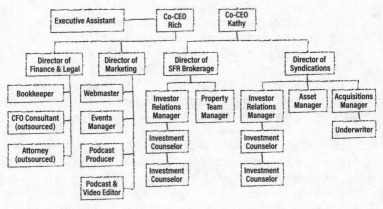

COMPARE CHARTS

Next, compare your two charts—current and future. Is there anything you should change now instead of waiting three years? Talk it over with your group and don't shy away from a bit of discomfort.

Then bring more people into the discussion—maybe your leadership team and entire board of directors (if you have one). Walk them through your charts, both current and future, and gather their input.

This whole process should take a couple of hours. It works best in person, in front of a whiteboard. If you tack this onto an in-person leadership meeting, wrap it up with a good meal after. You all deserve it!

As the owner and/or CEO, make sure that everything gets recorded—snapping photos with a phone is a great way to do this. Put it aside for a week, then revisit and plan out how you'll transition from your current org structure to the one you envision having three years down the road.

Yes, this takes a lot of mental energy—and it's worth it! You and your team will gain new clarity about where your company is today, how it's structured, what's working, what's not working, what needs attention, and what your company can look like in the future after you continue to scale it the smart way to maximize your wealth and freedom.

IDENTIFY YOUR NEXT HIRES (OR PROMOTIONS)

Now that you have a better idea of what your future business structure will look like, take some time to review the positions that may take care of the following issues.

- Bring in someone with solid experience
- Replace yourself with someone even better than you for that job, which would free up your time and energy for leadership
- Replace someone who is not a culture fit or is a low performer
- Launch a new product or service

When you proactively identify potential future hires for your business, you can also avoid last-minute hiring scrambles. By planning ahead, you can make sure you have the position and job description dialed in, which can save you from making a rushed decision. Plus, when you plan your hires in advance, you'll be more likely to find people who are a better fit with your current team. This can translate to happier and more effective employees who stick around for the long term.

The clearer you are on what your company needs to take it to the next level, the faster you'll find that person. Your focus becomes your reality.

Once you are clear on what you need, your brain's reticular activating system (see Chapter 8) will see it.

Knowing who you want to hire in the near future also allows you to skill up. You'll be prepared to onboard your new hire by investing in their training and development *before* they begin, so they'll be able to hit the ground running. This will help you put systems in place or hire someone who knows how to do that.

Finally, proactive hiring is all about supporting your business's big-picture purpose, mission, vision, and strategy. It helps ensure your staffing aligns with your growth plans and long-term goals.

Getting clear on your future hiring is a smart move for your business. It allows you to identify who needs to be hired and what skills and strengths that person should have. It helps you plan ahead, save money, keep your team happy, and stay competitive. It also means you'll make thoughtful hires that will contribute to your company's success in the long run, so you can focus on your true strengths and passions and be the leader your company needs to grow wisely.

And remember, if all of this sounds overwhelming, perhaps your first hire is finding someone who is great at hiring.

TAKEAWAYS

▶ Creating a business structure will help you figure out exactly who you need to hire full time or part time, as well as who might already be in your company but not in the right position.

▶ An organizational chart is a snapshot of the structure and reporting relationships within your company. It shows how different departments and teams are interconnected.

▶ When you create your first org chart, you may be handling multiple roles in your company, and that's okay. Over time, you'll be able to hire people to take over those roles, freeing you to focus on your unique strengths and contributions to the company.

- ▶ Don't bring in people who are affordable but not really qualified for the job. Hire people who can truly get you where you want to be, even if it's part time at first.
- ▶ It's so important to "know thyself and know thy team." The more diverse your team's abilities, the quicker you'll be able to scale.
- ▶ Don't try to mold your current team into the puzzle pieces you need. It's far more effective to determine which pieces are needed and then hire accordingly.
- ▶ Proactive hiring is about supporting your business's big-picture purpose, mission, vision, and strategy. It helps ensure your staffing aligns with your growth plans and long-term goals.
- ▶ Organizational charts should be fluid. They change constantly as the company grows. Your org chart may need to be reviewed and updated quarterly.

CHAPTER 6
SCALING YOUR TEAM OF SPECIALISTS

The difference between skill and talent: A skill is something you learn. Talent is what you can't help doing.

—CAROLINE GHOSN, FOUNDER AND CEO, LEVO

For you to be able to focus on your natural talents—those things you love and can't help doing—you'll need to hire others who have the skills needed for your company's offerings, operations, and management.

Sometimes those hires are part-time or full-time employees. We will discuss how to recruit, hire, and lead those awesome people in Part III: It's About the People.

But there are situations—especially in the earlier years of your business—when hiring someone with specialized knowledge and experience may break your budget, or when you might not be able to find everything you need in one person.

Many positions in a company can be outsourced, depending on the nature of the work and the company's specific needs. Outsourcing to part-time independent contractors, consultants, and companies can be a cost-efficient way to access specialized skills or handle tasks that are not core to your company's operations. These specialists can help you run your business more effectively, thanks to their deep knowledge and experience in their field.

For example, you can hire an Airbnb consultant on Upwork or Fiverr to help optimize a pricing app like PriceLabs. This consultant can dramatically increase your returns, for as low as $45. You can hire a social media expert to increase your following of ideal clients. You can bring on a part-time construction project manager to oversee your renovations, or find a bookkeeper on BELAY Solutions who you hire for just a few hours per week.

In this chapter, we're going to share what has worked for us at Real-Wealth, and for several other companies we researched and interviewed for this book, when it comes to filling roles with outsourced specialists.

WHY OUTSOURCE?

Outsourcing business professionals can be a real game changer for your company. Here are some key reasons why businesses often choose to outsource specialists, and the value they can bring.

- **Expertise:** Business specialists usually have expert knowledge in their field. By outsourcing, you can tap into this expertise without having to hire and train in-house staff, which can save you a lot of time and resources.
- **Scalability:** As your business grows, outsourcing can accommodate increased workloads or new projects without the need for extensive hiring and training.
- **Savings:** Outsourcing can save you some serious cash compared to hiring full-time employees. You can often find top talent in countries where labor is cheaper, which means you're not breaking the bank.
- **Focus on your strengths:** Let's face it—you're good at what you do. Outsourcing allows you and your team to stay in your own lanes while the specialists handle what they're good at.
- **More flexibility:** Outsourcing provides flexibility in scaling your business up or down as needed. You can easily ramp up or downsize your outsourcing as your needs change.
- **Access to global talent:** Outsourcing allows you to access talent from around the world, giving you access to specialists with a variety of backgrounds and experiences.
- **Less administrative hassle:** Managing in-house employees can be time consuming in terms of HR, payroll, benefits, and other administrative tasks. Outsourcing can minimize these duties.
- **Gain access to technology and tools:** People and companies you outsource to often have access to the latest technologies and tools in their fields, which can also improve your business operations.
- **Find A-players:** Many specialists have years of experience, which can lead to higher-quality work. Plus, they often have well-designed systems in place to make sure the work they do is top-notch.

Just remember, the value of outsourcing specialists can vary based on your business needs, the quality of the people you're outsourcing to, and the types of tasks being outsourced. It's important to carefully assess your goals and requirements, choose the right outsourced person or company, and establish clear communication and expectations based on your specific situation to maximize the value of outsourcing.

WHO CAN YOU HIRE?

You can outsource a number of jobs to part-time independent specialists or even entire companies who have a full team of experts. This can be a smart way to tap into specific skills without committing to the cost or management of full-time hires. The list below gives you a better idea of the different positions that can be outsourced.

- **Financial professionals:** Bookkeeping, accounting, and financial analysis can be managed by part-time independent contractors. At our company, we have a full-time director of finance who has been with us for fifteen years. We outsource with part-time experts, who help our finance director with bookkeeping, as well as a fractional CFO company, which helps our leadership team better understand how we are doing and where we are headed. Our leadership team meets with our outsourced CFO each month to review a multipage spreadsheet that none of us would have been able to create on our own.

- **Business coaches:** A business coach can play a pivotal role in enhancing your company's performance and profitability. Often, smaller and midsize businesses lack the internal resources and alignment required to navigate this complex journey, making the guidance of a coach indispensable. Whether you need to revitalize an existing business plan or start from scratch, the coach ensures that you stay on track and accountable.

  Ultimately, the result of their efforts is a clear, comprehensible operating system that can seamlessly integrate across all facets of your organization, contributing to improved efficiency and overall success. Even though Rich has been a certified business coach for more than twenty-five years, he still meets with his own coach once a month to help him grow, stay focused, challenge his limiting beliefs, and consistently become a better version of himself.

  We also know the importance of having someone from outside our business help us see things differently and look at how we can improve as a team and as a company. We have a full-day meeting every quarter with our coach, Dan Coleman, and host a two-day off-site planning meeting once a year. There are also many times when we'll call Dan for a quick coaching session on whatever specific issue needs to be addressed. Working with your own business coach can be one of your greatest assets in scaling smart and running smoothly.

- **Virtual assistants:** For tasks like managing emails, scheduling appointments, and handling data entry, virtual assistants can be a big help. We initially used a company that specialized in providing top-quality, experienced virtual assistants on a part-time basis for other companies. We liked our assistant so much that we decided to "buy her out" from that company, so she could come and work for RealWealth full time. By outsourcing, we were able to first see how she worked before deciding to hire her as a full-time employee.

- **Content creators:** If you need blog posts, articles, or marketing materials, freelance writers and content creators have got you covered. There are entire companies that focus on helping businesses create content, so the business can concentrate on taking care of their customers.

- **Graphic designers:** Whether it's a professional logo or eye-catching marketing visuals, independent graphic designers can bring your brand to life. There are multiple websites where you can search for skilled graphic designers, read their reviews, and even check out their portfolios before hiring them as an independent contractor. Oftentimes, when you find a good one, you'll keep that partnership going for a long time. We sure have!

- **Web designers and developers:** Building and maintaining websites or working on specific web projects can be handled by freelance web developers and designers. We worked with several independent companies to build our websites. Then, after we found the best company and worked with them for a few years, we hired the top talent when that company decided to close its doors.

- **Social media specialists:** They can help you with managing your social media accounts, strategizing, creating content, and running ad campaigns. Just be sure they truly know your brand and your voice. We once hired a specialist who didn't know anything about real estate investing, so it was difficult for them to really speak to our ideal audience. We then decided to hire our own full-time employee who understood investing and was committed to learning everything about what we do, why we do it, how we help people, and what makes us unique.

- **Marketing specialists:** Experts in search engine optimization (SEO), digital marketing, and online advertising can help boost your online presence. When Rich's first book came out, he hired a company that specialized in book promotion. They brought a ton of industry-specific knowledge that no one on our team knew or would have been able to figure out in time for his book's launch and follow-up promotional campaign.
- **Customer service:** Skilled independent contractors can provide remote customer support via phone and email.
- **Sales and lead generators:** If you need more sales leads, freelancers can help with cold calls, market research, following up with past customers, and more.

This is just a partial list of the different types of business specialists you could work with to help scale your business. There are specialists for just about any type of job in your organization. You can even hire a part-time CEO, COO, integrator, and more. If you are looking to grow your team of A-players but you don't want to grow your business broke in the process, outsourcing some specific jobs might be the solution for you.

HOW WE HIRED A WHOLE TEAM OF HR AND PAYROLL EXPERTS

About eight years ago, we were telling one of our business mentors how much time, energy, and people power it took to manage our payroll, benefits, human resources policies, and all that fun stuff. We wanted to focus on what we do best—helping investors improve their financial intelligence and grow their real estate portfolios. Instead, several people on our team (including Rich) were spending way too much time dealing with the endless details of government regulations related to employees.

Our mentor suggested that we look into a PEO. "A what?" we asked. Even though we had been entrepreneurs for decades, we had never heard of it.

He explained that a professional employer organization, or PEO, is a company that provides human resources (HR) services and support to other businesses. PEOs are often used by small and midsize businesses to help manage various HR-related tasks and responsibilities, allowing them to focus on their core business activities.

If you want, a PEO can also handle your payroll processing, employee benefits program (including health insurance, retirement plans, and other perks), workers' compensation, legal compliance and support, employee relations, and just about anything related to human resources.

We are grateful our mentor suggested that we work with a PEO. It has ensured that we are fully compliant with all labor laws and has saved us countless hours in payroll, benefits processing, and administration.

By partnering with a PEO, your business can access a wide range of HR expertise and services, often at a lower cost than hiring and maintaining an in-house HR person or team. PEOs can also help your business scale and adapt to changing HR and regulatory requirements, making them a valuable resource if you want to focus on your core operations and still have effective HR management.

HOW WE HIRED A WHOLE TEAM OF LAWYERS

As our company continued to scale over the years, we found that some people would name us in a lawsuit—even when we were not directly involved in whatever they had filed a suit for. When we asked an attorney why were were being named in lawsuits that we had nothing to do with, he replied, "Because the other companies named in the suit don't have the money. They named you in this lawsuit because you appear to have the bigger pockets." (No pun intended, BP!)

We would go through the lawsuit, do the depositions, and pay over $100k in legal fees. Then our attorney suggested that we just settle with the litigants rather than going to court because that would cost us another $50k and, even though he was very confident that we'd win the case, we wouldn't be able to recoup our legal fees from the other party. He said, "This is not about who is right or wrong, or going to court just to prove you're right. This is a business decision based on what's best for your company financially."

Even though we were getting more and more angry at the people who added us to their lawsuit just for having the "big pockets," we took our attorney's advice. Looking back, we're glad he shared that wisdom with us. It was a lesson that cost us over $100k, but it also taught us (in a painful way) the importance of having high-quality errors and omissions (E&O) insurance and having a general counsel attorney to make sure we hande any heated situation correctly from the get-go. That has helped us avoid lawsuits altogether.

We began working with a company that supplies outsourced, independent attorneys. We don't have to pay a salary for a full-time general counsel attorney, which would be very expensive. We simply reach out to our outsourced attorney whenever we have a legal question. The bonus is that our attorney has a whole team of other attorneys at his firm who can help us with their own unique talents and expertise, such as contract law, trademark law, and real estate law.

The last time we were named in a lawsuit, our general counsel immediately jumped on it and had our company removed from the frivolous lawsuit. That saved us from going down a much more expensive route to defend ourselves. Having an outsourced legal firm ready to help was one of the smarter business moves we have made.

Thousands of companies rely on freelance lawyers and part-time associates for legal know-how and to reduce overhead and increase profit. Your outsourced, part-time general counsel can act as the coordinator of all your company's legal activities and is often available as needed by phone, video conference, or on-site visit. They provide legal advice, contract solutions, risk management, and even process improvement to keep your company safe and solid. More importantly, they can review your processes to make it easier to have you dismissed from frivolous lawsuits in the future.

STAYING LEGAL WHEN OUTSOURCING YOUR CONTRACTORS

Be sure to stay on the right side of the law and taxes—both for your state and the IRS—when you're bringing in independent contractors.

If you are paying someone as a 1099 independent contractor to try to avoid payroll taxes, workers' comp, health insurance, paid time off, and more, you should understand the rules about what truly makes someone an independent contractor and when the tax authorities investigate how you are operating. If you do it wrong, it could add up to paying out more than you planned, plus possible penalties and fines.

If you're trying to save money by hiring someone as an independent contractor, make sure you're not their only client. Or, if you are their only client, that you don't employ them for more than six months. Then they may have to become a regular W-2 employee to avoid breaking the rules in your state or with the IRS.

Note that we aren't legal experts. You need to talk to your general counsel attorney, CPA, and/or HR specialist to make sure you're staying legit. If you don't have general counsel at your company, maybe that should be your next outsourced specialist.

Hiring Fractional Business Professionals

BiggerPockets CEO Scott Trench told us that he fully supports the use of fractional help.

"Don't be afraid to use a fractional, part-time executive. I've hired a fractional CFO, fractional HR leader, fractional CTO, and fractional Head of Product, and will absolutely use fractional leaders in the future when encountering new situations. All these folks have been able to lead the divisions they were assigned to, and that gave me time and space to make a cool, calm, and collected decision in hiring the right long-term executive for a full-time position. All go into the job knowing their role is to have the division perform, demonstrate some best practices, and give me room to hire a full-time replacement. Occasionally, the fractional executive will even apply for the full-time job, like in the case of our CTO, Kevin McGuire.

"For a much lower cost and lower risk profile than a full-time hire, I get to experiment and learn what 'good' is from executives who are not looking for a full-time gig and know their field inside and out. Many of these fractional leaders had huge company exits or success stories, or are decades into a successful career, hence not needing or wanting a new full-time job."

OUTSOURCING IS GOOD FOR THE SKULL

We'll wrap up this chapter with a success story on the power of outsourcing.

Let's rewind to 2003, when Rick Alden, the brains behind the tech company Skullcandy, was chilling on a chairlift in Park City, Utah. Picture this: He's jamming to some tunes on his headphones when suddenly, his phone rings. Now, back in the day, you had to do a whole song and dance to answer a call—take off the headphones, pause the MP3 player, dig out the phone, and finally answer it.

Rick thought, *This is way too much hassle*, and that's when the idea for Skullcandy was born. He came up with a genius headphone jack that could handle both the phone and the MP3 player simultaneously, plus a switch to toggle between them. And just like that, Skullcandy was in business, creating a perfect blend of music, fashion, and action-sports vibes. Their brand and iconic logo screamed youth and rebellion, perfectly summing up their motto: "Every revolution needs a soundtrack."

Skullcandy's products spread like wildfire, not just in the U.S., but also in over seventy countries around the globe. They were the pioneers of selling headphones catering to action sports and the young crowd. This helped them reach those trendsetters who gave the brand its street cred. And they didn't stop there—they expanded their reach to consumer electronics, mass retailers, sporting-goods shops, and even mobile-phone stores.

Now, here comes the twist: As Skullcandy was gearing up for some serious growth, they needed to get their financial act together. Initially, all their accounting records were jumbled up in Rick's personal bank account, handled by his wife. Talk about a DIY operation! They also knew they needed access to capital and a partner to guide them through this exciting phase.

THE GAME PLAN

Enter Ampléo, the same outsourced CFO firm that we use at RealWealth. Once they teamed up with Skullcandy, Ampléo helped Rick untangle the business from his personal finances. They got things sorted with inventory, purchases, and collections—you know, the nitty-gritty stuff. Over five years, Ampléo went all in. They provided Skullcandy with a controller and CFO, who helped them set up their first accounts-receivable factoring line, score some sweet equity capital from local angel investors, forecast cash flows, and boost operational growth. And guess what? Skullcandy skyrocketed, with revenue growth hitting over 7,200 percent, often exceeding an annual growth rate of more than 300 percent.

Ampléo didn't stop there—they even helped Skullcandy get their first traditional bank line of credit with Zions Bank, just a few months after they turned their first profit. The CFO from Ampléo became Rick's go-to strategic finance partner, always on speed dial for those important meetings where big decisions were made. When Skullcandy's growth demanded a full-time CFO, Ampléo stepped up to the plate, helping with the recruitment process, presenting multiple qualified candidates, and sealing the deal.

AND THEY LIVED HAPPILY EVER AFTER

Skullcandy's journey didn't stop there. In 2011, they went public with a whopping valuation of $500 million and started trading on the Nasdaq (SKUL). Now, that's what you call an outsourcing success story!

NEXT UP: BUILDING YOUR A-TEAM

In the next section, we'll cover hiring A-players, leading your team effectively, giving them the power to excel in their roles, and more. You'll learn how to create a workplace where your employees feel like they are part of your vision, key players in driving your business to success, and making a significant impact in your industry and community.

By focusing on these areas, you'll learn how to foster an environment where being great is just part of the job.

TAKEAWAYS

▶ If you can't afford the most qualified people for your company, it's okay. You can hire a skilled professional part time, as a consultant, or as an "outsourced" C-suite exec. The amount of money you spend will be far less in the long run than hiring someone full time who doesn't know what they're doing and is learning on the job.

▶ When you're thinking about whether to outsource a certain job, make sure to take a good look at the kind of work it involves, the skills required, and your company's budget.

▶ Many different positions can be outsourced to independent contractors—financial analysts, business coaches, virtual assistants, content creators, sales lead generators, and more.

▶ Outsourced legal firms often have decades of experience, are qualified to handle just about any legal issue or situation, and can work with your leadership team to identify and evaluate the situations that could impact your business.

▶ It's important to know the labor laws for both your state and the IRS when you're hiring independent contractors. Consult your general counsel attorney and follow all the rules.

PART III
IT'S ABOUT THE PEOPLE

CHAPTER 7

PERSONAL LEADERSHIP

Leaders should never be satisfied. They must always strive to improve, and they must build that mindset into the team. They must face the facts through a realistic, brutally honest assessment of themselves and their team's performance. Identifying weaknesses, good leaders seek to strengthen them and come up with a plan to overcome challenges ... It starts with the individual and spreads to each of the team members until this becomes the culture, the new standard.

—JOCKO WILLINK, AUTHOR, *EXTREME OWNERSHIP: HOW U.S. NAVY SEALS LEAD AND WIN*

"You say you want our input, but then you just take control and do things your way. You talk about teamwork, but you never support it!"

That was just one of the many complaints I (Rich) heard from team members of an engineering company in Silicon Valley about their CEO when I was facilitating their annual two-day retreat. The CEO had hired me to help the leadership team build out their annual plan and give them a team-building exercise on day one to help develop camaraderie among the company of eighty-five employees.

THE SPIDERWEB EXERCISE

For the team-building event, I set up a "spiderweb" exercise, with PVC pipes and string to create what looked like a large spiderweb about six feet wide and six feet tall. The web was woven with several large openings that were big enough for a good-size human body to go through. I told the team, "This side of the web is where you are. It's where your business is and where your team has been operating from. That side of the web [*pointing to the opposite side*] is where you want to be, both with your business goals and your strength as a team. This will be a timed event, and the objective is to get each member of your team through the web without touching any of the string. You can't walk around the sides of the web or go over the top. Those are the only rules. Just get all your team members from this side of the web to that side with no one touching the string. If anyone touches the web, then you all die and you have to start over."

Of course, someone asked how much time they had to complete the challenge. I smiled and replied, "You'll know when the time is up." In truth, saying they had a deadline was only to create a similar experience to the business world, where we know there's usually a deadline. I wanted the group to perform under pressure.

When everyone was ready, I started the timer and the team got to work. One agile person was able to step through a large hole in the net and make it through to the other side, with a couple of his team members guiding his second leg through the web so he wouldn't touch the string. Once he was on the other side, he'd be able to hold the hand of the next person, who stepped through with support from the team on the other side. Some smaller people tightened up their bodies like a stiff board, and their team slowly lifted and shuffled them through the larger opening in the web.

Once more than half the team had made it through, I looked at my watch and stated, "Remember, this is a timed event." Everyone got a little frantic, and confusion set in. They were trying to come up with a way to get the last few people through the web when the CEO exclaimed, "I know! Watch this!" He walked toward the web and tore it apart, leaving PVC pipes and a mess of string on the ground. I paused, looked at the CEO, and said, "Well, you just killed each person on your team. This exercise is over."

That's when people started to speak up, accusing the CEO of always saying they needed more teamwork but then making unilateral decisions that made every project more difficult and made the team feel like they were being told what to do, rather than asking the team for solutions to new challenges. The team was so frustrated that several people stepped forward and got very real, accusing the CEO of not walking his talk and not being a good leader. As he listened to the feedback, you could see the tension building in his demeanor and his red face.

This CEO had tried to fix the team, but instead, he killed it. He couldn't register the feedback. His ego couldn't take it. Had he paused, asked his team some questions, listened for ideas, and had effective conversations, this could have been a transformational experience.

I wish I could report that the CEO embraced the feedback from his team. Had he put his ego aside, he could have learned to be a better leader, which would have helped bring his whole company to a new level. Instead, I got an email from the CEO's assistant that evening letting me know the CEO didn't want me to come back for the second day because he was going to take over leading the annual event.

The CEO wanted to fix his team, but it became evident that *he* was the actual problem.

YOUR COMPANY IS A REFLECTION OF YOU

If your team isn't functioning well, don't look at the team, look at the leader. Your company is a reflection of you. It's that simple. If you don't like the way your company or team is performing, first look at yourself. Your company's performance, or lack thereof, is simply a mirror of where you are lacking or underperforming.

This doesn't mean you have to flog yourself for not being perfect. No one is perfect, and even if you're close, there are always ways to improve further. However, if we are blind to our shortcomings or refuse to look at them, we can't make changes.

The good news is there are many ways to support your growth as a leader. Leadership comes naturally for some people, but for most, it can be developed through learning, practice, mentoring, getting feedback, and—most of all—a willingness to admit that you don't have it all figured out, but you're committed to mastering this vital skill for guiding your team to a better future.

BE OPEN TO GETTING BETTER

When I (Kathy) taught acting lessons, I would record my students and replay their performances for them. That usually resulted in a lot of groans, but it also gave them a clear picture of ways they could improve. I hardly had to do any teaching at all. The video feedback was the teacher.

However, when I ventured into public speaking, I refused to watch myself. I didn't want to know how bad I was at it. But I was in awe of how Rich would study videos of his speaking, skiing, surfing, and anything else he wanted to improve. Eventually, I forced myself to painstakingly critique my speaking and podcast performances. And thankfully, over time, it got easier to accept my shortcomings and areas for improvement.

Bottom line, as we get better at being leaders, our companies get better. It starts with *you*. It's worth the discomfort. You just have to get yourself to the next level, and your team should follow. However, if some employees don't level up along with you, they will stand out and either leave of their own volition or it will be easier to let them go—especially after you've given them several clear warnings that are not adhered to.

WHAT DO WE MEAN BY "NEXT LEVEL?"

Let's start with a real-life—and obvious—example of what is *not* next-level leadership.

Our company is always vetting real estate brokers and investment property companies. Our business model is to refer clients to brokers and builders nationwide who can provide quality rental properties to our members. Before we make the referral, we want to get to know the leaders of these brokerages and builder teams We found that hanging out with people outside of work is one of the best ways to discover who they *really* are.

On one occasion, we took a business owner out to dinner. We had some drinks, and some interesting information came out: This company owner had a taste for cocaine and pursuing the ladies. Enough said.

We did not engage with this company after that, as we believed this kind of behavior wouldn't stay out of the business (plus we didn't condone his actions in general). Sure enough, we later learned through the grapevine that the boardroom was used for lines and ladies—yes, during the day, every day. It didn't take long to find out the company had overspent, and the owner was out of the country and could not come back due to pending lawsuits.

While it's obvious that a company leader who is addicted to drugs and sex might end up sinking the ship, it illustrates how much a leader's personal habits and actions influence the company—creating a team culture of disrespect for the leadership as well as embarrassment to work for the company, the crumbling of standards due to excessive permissiveness and lack of boundaries, and so on.

What's more difficult to assess is the less obvious. An example might be a company that is not hitting its goals because the leader is too relaxed and doesn't prioritize those goals or doesn't even have goals. Or maybe the company's employees get burned out because a leader has too many goals. These are all situations that point to poor or weak leadership.

On the flip side are next-level leaders, people who are committed to growing into the best leaders they can be. You can become a better leader when you decide to become a better leader. When you "walk the talk" of good leadership, you inspire other leaders at your company to step up their game. They are inspired by how you operate. They are constantly watching you to see how you show up, how you handle challenges, how you communicate, and how well you respect yourself and your team. And it all begins with your frame of mind.

GOOD LEADERSHIP STARTS WITH MINDSET

Way back in 1995, we (Rich and Kathy) met each other in a personal-growth workshop. Each of us separately signed up for that ninety-day program because we were told it would help us increase our income and live a better life. What we didn't realize was that the workshop was focused on personal leadership. What they promoted—more money and a better life—are the truth of what happens when you develop yourself as a leader.

During the first weekend of that workshop, we learned the power of the "I am" statement. It turns out that whole spiel wasn't just sales talk; it was about the real magic that happens when you start leading yourself.

Let's talk about "I am." It's short, but it packs a punch. Saying "I am" is like giving yourself a secret superpower, especially when you tack on "a leader."

When you begin to think of yourself as a leader, you begin to act like a leader. As personal development speaker and author Earl Nightingale said many years ago, "We become what we think about day and night."[13] That is how mindset shifts happen. When you start to think, *I am a leader*, there is a permanent shift in how you see yourself, and then everything else starts to change. Once you have a true mindset shift, it's tough to see things the way you previously did.

When you commit to being an effective leader, magic starts to happen: You become aware of other effective leaders. You start to notice books, articles, and podcasts about leadership, and you might even find other leaders you respect showing up in your social media feeds.

Being an effective leader isn't about bossing people around; it's about being that person everyone looks up to and respects. Someone kind, humble, grounded, inspirational, open to learning, and who lifts others up. That kind of leadership is pure gold.

---

13 Earl Nightingale, *The Strangest Secret* (Merchant Books: 2013).

LEARNING LEADERSHIP

How do we become better leaders? After setting the intention and stating that you are a leader, then you can go to work on learning leadership the same way you improve at most things—through study, mentoring, coaching, practice, and experience.

There is an endless amount of information out there on how to be a better leader. A quick search on Amazon for "leadership books" shows that there are more than 50,000 books on the topic! But reading about leadership is just the start. It's like learning to ride a bike: You can read all you want about bicycling, but until you sit on that seat and start peddling, you're not going to become a good bike rider.

When you learn something new or inspiring about leadership, put it into practice right away. See what works for you and what doesn't.

Another way to improve your leadership skills is to hang out with leaders you respect. When we asked Tarl Yarber, CEO of Fixated Real Estate and Fixated Events, how he became a quality leader, he told us:

"There has been nothing more true in my life than who you hang around determines who you become. I heard this for years growing up and at one point lumped it in with all the other euphemisms out there. Then, in my late twenties, I had real-world evidence and experience that made me realize how true this statement is. If you want to be a better leader, start hanging out with better leaders. If you want to be better with investing, hang out with people who are better at investing. If you want to be a better human, start hanging out with better humans."

What about you? Are you hanging out with great leaders who are constantly learning and practicing how to be better leaders? If not, look for professional networking groups you can join. There are plenty of them in most cities. If you can't find one you like, consider starting one! You can also get active in BiggerPockets community forums that are filled with business leaders offering mentorship. And library shelves and bookstores are full of business books that offer collegiate-level education for free or at a low cost.

Are you taking in information about or observing how to be a better leader? If so, your future self (and your team) will thank you for it. We guarantee it.

LEADERSHIP ISN'T JUST GIVING ORDERS

The more we learn about leadership, the more we've seen that being a great leader is like being a ship's captain, who do more than just yell orders; they set the direction, get everyone excited, and make sure everyone's on point. They're the decision-makers, the ones grabbing opportunities, and simply the type of people you want to be around.

Awesome leaders are also magnets for talented people. They make work into a place you want to be. When things get crazy—like with market fluctuations, tech glitches, people flaking, or a lawsuit out of nowhere—they're the ones keeping the team calm, grounded, and focused. They're all about adapting and finding smarter ways to do things, and inspiring their team to do the same.

Leaders earn trust and respect by setting high standards and walking the talk. Whether it's fixing problems or coming up with new ideas, their impact is huge.

Embrace your inner leader. Starting to see yourself as a leader is a huge step. It's as simple (and difficult) as saying "I am a leader" and really meaning it. This isn't just about your success; it's about the kind of leader you become and the leaders you help shape.

Notes on Being a Leader

Vicky Schiff is an industry-recognized real estate investment executive. Since 1996, she has successfully founded or cofounded six firms in various sectors of the real estate and private equity business. She started her sixth investment company in 2023. Vicky has been honored with industry awards by multiple organizations and publications, and she is an advocate for more women leaders and participants in the real estate investment industry.

"A leader must make decisions," she says, but they should also be able to step back and listen. "It's important to allow others to have input and make decisions. A leader doesn't have the time, nor is it good practice, to try to exert control over people or do their jobs for them. Rather, empower them to make decisions within a construct or business plan. Provide guidelines and let others utilize their creativity, drive, and talent to get things done, but leave the door open for guidance. Entrust people who have good judgment. Sometimes, even if I don't 100 percent agree, I have to let the right people execute and not be a control freak. If a leader has the wrong person in the wrong position or someone who is simply not working out, make changes quickly. You can't drag it on."

Vicky knows that effective leaders also make people feel valued. "Make sure people feel supported, are given credit for their work, and feel that they can respectfully speak freely in meetings, which allows them to flourish. Meetings should be structured with time limits, purposeful and short," she explains. "Meetings are to connect, to be in sync, to share ideas. Don't have too many meetings, and don't include people who aren't really involved."

Other leadership pointers? "Incentives are important. Be clear on goals. Maybe you measure quarterly or annually, and there's stated room for growth in terms of promotions. In a private-equity-type business, incentives such as long-term carried interest or profit participation drive alignment of interests and can be both inspiring and motivating. You want people to stick around and grow. One tool we used in the past, in addition to employee bonus programs, is to give a certain amount of money annually to the charity of a team member's choice. It's eye-opening and heartwarming what people care about."

Good leaders also get to know their team members personally. "Spend time one-on-one. Take them to lunch. Get to know them and what's important to them. Know their spouse's and children's names and what they are interested in," she advises. "If it's a senior or mid-level position, include spouses from time to time in company events or dinners to help them feel supported. If you understand what's important to someone outside of work, you'll understand what drives them."

YOUR MOST IMPORTANT ROLE AS A LEADER

What would you say is the most important role of a leader? Pause and think about that for a moment.

We have asked this question to friends, other company leaders, new employees, and participants in our mastermind retreats. We often hear "motivating and inspiring" or "being the one who charges ahead." Some people claim "setting the vision" while others say "decision-making."

We agree with all these answers. Leaders are responsible for setting a clear vision and direction for their team or organization. Leaders need to inspire and motivate their team members. Leaders need to be able to analyze situations, consider various perspectives, and make informed choices that benefit the group. They must also be adept at identifying problems, brainstorming solutions, and adapting to changing circumstances and challenges. Another significant role of a leader is to develop and mentor their team members.

However, when you boil it all down, we believe the most important role of a leader is having effective conversations. Whether that be one-on-one or in a state-of-the-company address to everyone in your organization, having effective conversations is vital.

What are effective conversations?

First, these are *not* where you sit in your office going over the books or working on a business plan or reading emails. This is where you need to make the shift from being a worker to being a leader.

Effective conversations are all about exchanging ideas, thoughts, opinions, and knowledge so the message is received and understood with clarity and purpose. When we communicate effectively, both the sender and the receiver feel heard and understood. When we have effective conversations, we help move our team forward with our goals and purpose. We connect with others who can bring new ideas, challenge how things are being done, create new plans, and provide feedback for smarter growth.

I (Rich) have my business coach ask me the following question every time we speak: "On a scale of 1 to 10, how well are you being a leader versus being a worker?"

Why that question? Because I know it's too easy to slip back into "tasky" work that gives me a quick feeling of progress or completion. By being aware of that, I can keep an eye on doing what truly matters for our company—having effective conversations with the other leaders and team members at RealWealth who are focused on our company's purpose, mission, vision, and goals. You won't find other leaders like Richard Branson, Elon Musk, or Mary Barra isolated in their offices creating reports or reading through countless emails. You'll find them meeting with the leaders at their companies or being ambassadors of their brands through effective conversations.

Of course, a leader has multiple roles, including guiding, inspiring, supporting their team toward a compelling vision, and much more. What we're saying is the *most important* role for making all of that happen well is to have effective conversations with your team members. Don't get stuck in the doing. Focus on leadership, and you'll help your company thrive.

THE VALUE OF HUMILITY, A HEALTHY ATTITUDE, AND SELF-AWARENESS

Start thinking of your business as a never-ending personal growth workshop that you can use to develop the qualities of a great leader.

Humility is one of those important qualities. AJ Osborne, CEO of Cedar Creek Capital, understands this. He is an entrepreneur, podcast host, and investor who manages a self-storage portfolio of over $212 million through his companies Cedar Creek Wealth, Bitterroot Holdings, and Clearwater Benefits. He explains that success isn't all about the founder.

"People think, first and foremost, that so much of their success is because of them. They don't realize where they are is partly due to luck, and they don't realize that much of their success is not due to *their* efforts, but the efforts of their team. Because they don't realize that, they get into trouble. I've experienced that personally, and I think that I've gotten in my own way plenty of times." AJ learned he needed to stay humble to become the good leader that he is today.

Some who boast about being natural leaders don't realize they might be natural narcissists. Remember the arrogant CEO in the spiderweb exercise and the repercussions he faced? It takes humility to lead a team without being a dictator. It takes humility to recognize that you can learn to be a better leader. It takes humility to want to learn and grow. Do you have that humility?

Another one of the proven, foundational traits of an effective leader is self-awareness and presence. Great leaders don't lose their head when things go wrong—instead, they know that's when their team needs them most.

It's vital to keep your attitude in check and develop the ability to stay calm under pressure. But how do you do that?

EFFECTIVE LEADERSHIP CAN BE FOUND IN "THE SPACE"

If you are a student of personal or business growth, you've probably seen Viktor Frankl's quote: "Between stimulus and response there is a space. In that space is our power to choose a response. In our response lies our growth and freedom."

Frankl was an Austrian psychiatrist and Holocaust survivor who wrote the best-selling book *Man's Search for Meaning*, which is based on his experiences in various Nazi concentration camps. What we believe Frankl meant in the above quote is that there will always be challenges, ranging from life-or-death (like being a prisoner in a Nazi concentration camp) to small ones—which can sometimes feel major—such as troublesome employees, a deal that fell through, someone ripping you off, someone cutting you off in traffic, you name it. What *really* matters is how you handle those challenges.

For example, if the "stimulus" was one of your employees completely messing up a project and then blaming your company for not giving them enough training, you could get upset, yell at them, defend your training process, or maybe even fire them out of anger. Or you could recognize the stimulus, notice that your blood is starting to boil, and then pause, take a deep breath, and ask yourself, *What is the most effective way to handle this?* Then you can choose your response.

This seems simple, but we know it's more challenging than it sounds. However, it does get easier over time. You develop the ability to notice when you are getting hooked and the ability to follow the process, turning you into a more effective leader. Instead of being that boss who gets angry and belligerent and says things that dissolve trust, you become a leader who is grounded, impactful, and inspiring. When people trust you as a leader, it's much easier to have those effective conversations, no matter who you are speaking with.

THE THREE LEVELS OF LEADERSHIP

AJ Osborne believes there are three tiers of leadership when scaling a business—first-degree, second-degree, and third-degree leadership—and the entrepreneur must keep evolving to rise to each new level.

"When you're first starting out, there is no degree of separation. You are working directly with your customers, so you are directly connected with them," he explains.

As your business grows, you'll hire employees to work with your customers, and eventually you'll hire managers to oversee those employees. This puts one degree of separation between you and some of your team.

"The first degree of leadership is not too difficult to muscle through because you can still step in and make up for any mistakes or weaknesses, with your team," says AJ. "You can overcompensate for their weaknesses and management isn't as important. It's commanding. Just tell them what to do."

As your business continues to scale, you'll reach the second degree of leadership, where you have to be an actual leader. "You have to discipline yourself to work on the business strategy, vision, and goals, and also empower your company's leaders to be better leaders for their direct reports," AJ explains. "You're not working directly with employees anymore. Your time is focused on scaling the business and being an effective leader for your managers."

Lastly, you have third-degree leadership. "You're not near the customer at all," AJ says. "You're not near your employees or even all your managers. You are now doing the overseeing of the executors, because they're dealing with the managers."

SECOND-DEGREE LEADERSHIP: THE LITMUS TEST

First-degree leadership comes with its shares of struggles. But the second degree of separation is where most entrepreneurs fail.

Sometimes the reason is a lack of systems and processes in the company, so each person is coming up with their own way of doing things rather than following a process that has been documented, tested, and improved over time.

However, the main reason leaders fail at this second level is because they haven't developed their skills and effectiveness as a leader. Team members aren't clear on their roles and responsibilities, and they're not clear and passionate about the company's purpose, mission, vision, values, and way of doing things.

When you're at the second-degree leadership level, you find out if you're truly a good business builder. If you haven't empowered your team to build the business on proven systems and processes, you'll see it. If people are fighting, disgruntled, or quitting, that's a strong sign that your leadership is failing.

But if you're willing to be humble, admit your mistakes and weaknesses, and learn how to grow yourself and find others who are committed to being great, effective leaders, you'll realize that you *are* becoming a good leader—and you'll begin to build a solid, thriving business.

THIRD-DEGREE LEADERSHIP: BEING A LEADER OF LEADERS

People who don't build a business on systems and processes fail—and people who don't develop a team of inspired leaders also fail.

When you're at the third degree of leadership, it means you have inspired leaders in your company who are now growing and scaling your business without you having to be hands-on. Your role shifts into helping set the vision for the future of your company and creating business plans and important goals with the help of those leaders. You are empowering your team to come up with new ideas and initiatives, to review the current way of doing things, and to figure out how to improve all areas of your business. You are involved in the high-level part of this strategy, but your company's leaders are focused on the execution of the strategy and vision.

When we asked AJ what his main role is at Cedar Creek Capital today, he replied, "I'm the visionary, and I have leaders who are the executors. The managers work with everything, so now I'm no longer focused on being an executor. Not only am I no longer an executor on the ground, I'm not even executing big things. Today, I am a creator of opportunity and resources for the management team. That way, they can execute, and I can focus on building the future of our business. I also need to continue to be allocating opportunities and capital into the best projects, people, and profits."

That's third-degree leadership. At this level, you are a leader of leaders. This can be very difficult for entrepreneurs to embrace. Some get stuck in first-degree or second-degree leadership because they lack the humility to understand they don't have all the answers. Third-degree leaders are totally different types of leaders, and many people can't transition into that level. But now that you're armed with the knowledge from this chapter, you can make that journey!

EVERYONE WANTS A GOOD LEADER

In Chapter 4, we talked about the importance of creating a strong company culture. It's a powerful realization knowing it will help you put your business on autopilot. The next vital awareness is that a strong company culture starts with you, the leader of the company.

Your team, your investors, your board of directors, and your customers all want you to be an effective leader. Everything you do as a business leader is constantly being observed. That can be intimidating or inspirational, depending on how you look at it. Choose the latter. Rise to the occasion.

TAKEAWAYS

▶ If you don't like the way your company or team is performing, first look at yourself. Your company's performance is a mirror of where you are lacking or underperforming.

▶ Deciding that you are a leader is the first step. Claim it. Then learn how to become a good leader through education, mentorship, and practice.

▶ It's vital to learn and grow yourself as a leader. When you get better, everything around you gets better.

- ▶ Personal leadership doesn't just happen. It's not natural for most people. It's like wisdom—it comes through experience, knowledge, and good judgment.
- ▶ Great leaders have humility, self-awareness, and presence. They know how to keep their attitude in check.
- ▶ Always be open to receiving feedback and learning new things. Be willing to admit that you don't have it all figured out.
- ▶ Your business is a never-ending personal growth workshop you can use to develop the qualities of a great leader.
- ▶ There are three levels of leadership: first-, second-, and third-degree. At the first degree, you're only one level removed from your employees. At the second degree, you're managing a team. At the third degree, you're a leader of leaders.

CHAPTER 8

RECRUITING AND ONBOARDING YOUR A-TEAM

It doesn't make sense to hire smart people and then tell them what to do; we hire smart people so they can tell us what to do.

—STEVE JOBS, COFOUNDER AND FORMER CEO, APPLE

If you want a business that eventually runs on autopilot, you'll need to scale your team. Every business, no matter the size or industry, thrives on the energy, talent, and passion of its employees. If you've got a great vision for your business and a plan to make it a reality, you need a dream team to support that plan.

This chapter is your guide for rounding up a squad that doesn't just clock in but also lifts your business to new heights. Let's look at how you can attract those A-players who can bring unique strengths to your company.

DO YOU REALLY NEED A GREAT TEAM?

As an entrepreneur, you probably have lots of great ideas for your business. You have a vision for your company and how your products or services can make a positive impact on the world. You can have the best idea ever—but if you don't have the right team to execute on that idea, it will most likely die.

A brilliant idea is like a spark, but it's your team that's going to fan that spark into a blaze. At RealWealth, we made a huge banner for our annual retreats that reads "The only thing more important than a great idea is the team that can see it through." It's the people who make the magic happen, turning "what if" into "what is."

To scale smart, you need a team of skilled specialists to help you achieve your ambitious goals. We have found the learning curve for generalists is too steep for today's fast and complex world. Teams need to be well rounded, but their individual members don't need to be.

Right People, Right Seats

Our business coach, Dan Coleman, says, "I often get asked, 'What's the common denominator of the most successful companies you've ever worked with?' And it's super simple: having the right people in the right seats.

"Right people, right seats, but in the right structure. Too many entrepreneurs don't take a holistic approach to fixing their business. It's put out this fire, try to hire fast for that. My advice is to take a holistic approach. Right people, right seats, doing the right things in the right structure.

"The best companies obsess over getting their teams right, because the best companies are a team of teams, starting with the leadership team. The best companies aren't shy about raising the floor on their standards, which raises the ceiling."

THE GAME PLAN FOR BUILDING YOUR DREAM TEAM

So, how do you put together a team that's in it to win it with you? Here's what we will cover in this chapter.

- **Team-building overview:** Why you need a great team and how to build one.
- **Recruiting:** Getting clear on what each job is to attract the ideal candidates and then showing them what makes your company a great place to work.
- **Hiring:** Keeping your interviewing process focused and effective and then choosing the right people, both in skills and culture fit.
- **Onboarding:** Rolling out the red carpet for new team members makes them feel like part of the family from the get-go and makes them want to stick around.

Let's dive into each step, so you can find the right people for your dream team.

TEAM BUILDING IN A NUTSHELL

Every business needs talented people to help it succeed. Your job is to build and develop that team, just like a football coach in charge of recruiting. The starting point is recognizing where the team needs support and then finding the talent to fill that void.

Before you begin to recruit for a position, you need to get very clear on the outcome you want from this new hire. Because every employee is an expense to the company, their job description should almost be treated as if it has its own business plan.

Start by determining the vision for this role, the cost (their salary and benefits), and the reward (how they can help the business save time and/or make more money). Then create a mission for the position. This should include the focus of the job, the key roles and responsibilities, and the desired outcomes for the person in that role. Once you've decided what outcomes you want from them, you can start homing in on the skills, experience, and personality of the person who would fit that role.

After you've hired your star players, the next step is properly onboarding and training them, so they'll integrate seamlessly into the company culture. When you imagine yourself as the head football coach, you realize you could never take credit for winning the game. Your team should get that honor. But you *can* take credit for assembling that team, offering the right coaching, and helping create the best systems and processes for success.

Finally, if you hope to someday let others take care of the daily operations of your company, you need to help your employees become leaders who take ownership of their roles and responsibilities. This requires empowering each person on your team to be the best they can be, to make the right decisions, and to take the necessary actions without always asking the person they report to or, even worse, you. You become a leader of leaders, as we discussed in the previous chapter.

Considering the costs of making a bad hire, it pays to get this hiring process right.

Building a Team: Moving from Generalists to Specialists

Jilliene Helman is a pioneer in real estate crowdfunding. In 2012, President Obama signed the Jumpstart Our Business Startups Act (aka the JOBS Act) into law, allowing private companies to publicly raise money and issue securities. Jilliene was just 25 years old at the time, but she saw the opportunity.

She created RealtyMogul, a technology platform that allows real estate operators to market their investments publicly. To date, as CEO of RealtyMogul and its wholly owned subsidiaries, Jilliene has been involved in investments with property values over $7 billion, including over 35,000 apartment and single-family units.

How was Jilliene able to scale her business so quickly when she had no real prior experience as a business owner?

In the beginning, like most small business owners, she hired generalists—people who are like Swiss Army knives: They can jump in and take care of any job needed in the company, even if they are hired for a specific role. She hired a great engineer who could also do product marketing. She had an underwriter who could also write blogs.

Jilliene says that the shift from running a small business to a large one is having the ability to move from hiring generalists to hiring specialists. Today, she has an engineering manager whose only focus is overseeing their state-of-the-art tech platform. The random marketing jobs that the former engineer did are now completed by specialists. She had one underwriter before who handled many tasks, but today she has acquisition managers, analysts, and asset managers, all of whom have a much more narrow and specialized focus.

"I'm a loyal CEO, yet in order for the company to scale, I had to make hard decisions," Jilliene says. "Generalists may not be the best specialists. It's hard to scale if you don't have the best person for the job, especially in a competitive field. Sometimes I had to replace the people who had helped me get the company started with people who were more qualified. I would still offer them a position in the company if there was a fit, but it might be for a lower-paying role. Most would exit, while some stayed. They all got stock options for their efforts in building the company."

Because Jilliene was a young and inexperienced CEO and couldn't afford an executive business coach, she read every business book she could get her hands on. One was *Mastering the Rockefeller Habits,* by Verne Harnish, a book that emphasizes the importance of transitioning from hiring generalists to only hiring specialists. Jilliene learned about the Functional Accountability Chart, which spells out who's responsible for which results—and every employee has a metric or company result they are responsible for.

"This means we have to come up with very clear job descriptions so that new employees know exactly what is expected of them," she says. "One of my first mistakes was building an expensive executive team before we were ready. That's how we got over our skis, with higher expenses than revenues. We had to eventually lay off many of those new hires. I learned that the company must earn new employees by hitting certain metrics first.

"Now, if we want to hire a new underwriter, that process starts ninety days prior and must be tied to milestones. That milestone might be that we hit a revenue goal, plus we have the training and onboarding materials built out. If those milestones aren't met, we don't unlock funding for the new hire.

"Part of the milestone for hiring a new person is having my team create a very specific job description that details all the duties and expectations of the job, including the challenging parts. No one knows those tasks better than people who are currently holding those roles, so they get involved in building out the job description for a new hire to either help them or replace them. The more detailed the better, so the new hire is not surprised by the workload when they come on board.

"In the early days, moving from generalist to specialist, we were not great at setting up a new hire with goals and specific roles, so we failed at meeting their expectations. There was a gap between what job they thought they were getting and the reality of it. Today, we've gotten really good at setting expectations. In fact, our interviews today are all about expectations, as we've found that happiness is the intersection of expectations and reality. Before putting out the job description, we ask our team if it properly describes the job today: the good, the bad, and the ugly."

RECRUITING: FINDING THE BEST CANDIDATES

To find the right people for your team, you'll need a clear recruitment process. The key components are:

- **Clear job description:** Articulate the roles and responsibilities clearly to attract the right candidates.
- **Employer branding:** Attract top talent by showcasing your company's culture, values, and growth opportunities.

- **Diverse sourcing channels:** Use a mix of sourcing channels including job boards, social media, referrals, and professional networks to reach a diverse candidate pool.
- **Assessment tools:** Implement tools and tests to evaluate the skills, cultural fit, and potential of candidates efficiently.

CLEAR JOB DESCRIPTION

When you are creating a job description, give lots of thought to the specific and measurable outcomes a potential hire needs to accomplish in their role. Start with what they need to achieve in the next year or two, and write that down.

For example, how much revenue does a salesperson need to bring in? Or how many new customers does your marketing manager need to attract? Or what type of systems does your financial manager need to develop this year?

Knowing these measurables will help you create a clear job description and think of specific questions to ask candidates during your interview process, so you can get more insight into their individual experience and the skills they can bring to your company.

The Power of the RAS

When you put a goal into your mind that is very specific, you are literally telling your brain what to search for. That is the power of the reticular activating system (RAS).

The RAS is a bundle of nerves at your brain stem that filter out the noise around you, so only the important stuff gets through. It works like a computer operating system in the background of your mind, helping you focus on and notice only the information relevant to you. Scientists believe that you can influence the RAS by focusing intently on your goals and outcomes.[14]

What does that mean for business owners trying to hire new employees? By getting absolutely clear on what you want in a hire, you will have a much better chance of finding—and recognizing—that person.

---

[14] Joseph H. Arguinchona and Prasanna Tadi, "Neuroanatomy, Reticular Activating System," StatPearls Publishing, July 24, 2023, https://www.ncbi.nlm.nih.gov/books/NBK549835/.

EMPLOYER BRANDING

Employer branding is all about showing off what makes your company a great place to work. It's not just about the products or services your company offers, but also its personality. This includes the vibe of the place (aka culture), what your company stands for (its values), and the perks of being part of the team, like opportunities to grow and learn.

Think of it as your company's way of saying "Hey, look how great we are to work for!" You use stories, images, and real employee experiences to paint a picture of life at your company. This can be shared on social media, your company's career page, or even at job fairs.

A big part of why employer brand matters is because people want to work someplace they feel good about, where they can get along with their colleagues, and where they see a future for themselves. If your company can show that it's not just another corporate machine—that it cares about its people and their growth—it can attract the right kind of talent. These are the people who are not only skilled but also a perfect fit for your company's culture and values.

DIVERSE SOURCING CHANNELS

When we started RealWealth, in 2003, the main way to find candidates for a job was through classified ads, because only one in five companies used online services for recruiting. In fact, it wasn't until 2003 that job seekers were even able to set up a LinkedIn profile! However, by the end of that decade, those numbers changed, as people became increasingly comfortable using the internet.

Today, there are numerous recruitment methods available, such as using social media, creating job postings, emailing your current list, and asking friends and colleagues for their referrals.

You can also use specialized software to find qualified candidates and then sort out who is the best of the applicants. Applicant tracking systems (ATS) are part of many of today's recruiting tools.

We recommend using Wizehire during your hiring process. It's an award-winning end-to-end hiring platform that marries innovative software with the hands-on expert support you need to grow your team with confidence. As of the writing of this book, over 18,000 businesses have used Wizehire to help grow their teams. That's what we now use for recruiting at RealWealth, and it has made all the difference for us. Our last job posting received more than 450 applicants, and we were able to use the Wizehire software to automatically ask all applicants further questions, have them take a DiSC® Assessment, and sort the applicants into different categories such as "completed all questions," "wow candidates," "already interviewed," and "on the short list."

Zoho Recruit is another all-in-one recruitment software that manages every aspect of your recruiting process, from job requisition and interview scheduling to finding the perfect match for any open role you have. You can find even more options with a quick internet search for applicant tracking systems.

Finally, keep your eyes and ears open—you never know where you might find your next great team member. It could even be someone you happen to meet in person.

Finding Leah

Just like with any goal, it's extremely helpful to get clear about the specific outcome you want to achieve when hiring talent. One goal we had at RealWealth was to hire another investment counselor who would not only be able to help our investors with their investing plans but would also be able to give presentations in front of a room full of people or on our weekly webinars. Ideally, we wanted someone who was heavily invested in rental properties in the markets we promote. This new hire seemed to be the last piece needed for both of us to take time away from the business, go on adventure trips, or travel with our family without having to carve out time during our trip to host a webinar from our hotel room or a local cafe.

We figured that finding the right person would be difficult, because we'd only hire someone who had the skills *and* would be a great fit for our RealWealth culture. We have a "quirky" culture based on a unique purpose of helping people create real wealth (having the money and the freedom to live life on their own terms). We're all about authentic connection, transparency, and a family-like vibe. And being in California, there's also a bit of "woo-woo," as we incorporate meditation, qigong, and yoga into our company retreats. We are the opposite of a typical corporate structure—and that culture has served us well over the past twenty years.

Most importantly, this recruit would need to have a heart for our investors, putting them before our own profits. Integrity is our most important value.

We discussed what characteristics and skill sets we would want in this new hire and then planned to put the job out there as we had in the past: by emailing our list of over 70,000 members to let them know we had a job opening available (this was long before we started using Wizehire). If we didn't find someone that way, we'd turn to other methods, such as social media and online hiring platforms.

Soon afterward, we held a live event in the San Francisco Bay Area. Part of the event was an investor panel featuring four different couples who had each invested together. We wanted them to share their lessons learned, their challenges, and their wins. Kathy was moderating the panel and asked questions such as "What has been one of the most important lessons you've learned about investing out of state?" and "If you could go back and do things differently, what would you change?"

As each couple replied, one of them piqued Kathy's interest. Leah was knowledgeable, eloquent, and passionate about investing. Plus, she had a great, positive vibe. Rich had interviewed Leah and her husband, Preston, earlier that day for a video we were creating for our website to help educate and inspire other investors. Rich was equally impressed with both Leah and her husband.

After the event, we shared our thoughts on Leah. Kathy said, "Imagine having Leah as an investment counselor!" It wasn't just Leah's words but her passion for investing that resonated with us and, by extension, with our audience.

Rich agreed. "You should talk to her!"

Kathy reached out to Leah, thanked her for being on the panel, and then asked, "Is there any chance you'd be interested in working at RealWealth?"

Leah was blown away. She said, "Oh wow … I was just telling Preston that same thing!"

After a few conversations and a little due diligence from both Leah and us, she became our newest investment counselor. It turned out she also had broadcast experience and was able to take over as host of our webinars and emcee of our live events. Several months after that, Leah had shown so much initiative, knowledge, investing experience, and passion that we elevated her to be the director of our real estate brokerage.

Thankfully, she is still an investment counselor today because she loves helping people one-on-one. But she is now also a vital part of our leadership team. For us at RealWealth, finding Leah was like discovering a needle in a haystack, a story that underscores the essence of building a dream team.

Why do we share this story? Again, it's the value of being clear and specific about your goals. Had we not gotten clear on what we wanted for a next hire, we might not have even recognized Leah that day.

ASSESSMENT TOOLS

Getting the right people on your team requires knowing how they tick. Tools like the Kolbe A™ Index and DiSC® Assessment, which we'll discuss below, can help you better understand how someone approaches tasks and how their personality jells with your team's mojo. This kind of insight is gold when you're looking to match tasks with temperaments.

KOLBE A INDEX: HOW EACH PERSON APPROACHES THEIR WORK

The Kolbe A™ Index (Instinct Assessment) is unique. It does not assess intelligence, personality, or social style; it instead measures the instinctive ways people do things. You can use the custom Kolbe A™ Index results to better understand what makes an individual more productive, more effective, less stressed, and more joyful at work.

Knowing how people act on a project can be valuable when delegating the right project to the right person. For example, salespeople often don't have the strength, skills, or desire to take on a big project that is going to take a lot of planning, research, or focused work. They usually like to have goals to hit. They love to play the game of sales, and they love to win. On the opposite side of the spectrum, people in financial management, such as bookkeepers, accountants, or CFOs, likely perform better in their roles when they can focus on fact-finding, analyzing, and creating and following a proven system and processes.

This is where the Kolbe assessment can help shed some light, by showing you how potential hires and current employees will act with their assigned roles and responsibilities.

DISC ASSESSMENT: EACH PERSON'S UNIQUE PERSONALITY

You may already know that there are many personality tests for hiring candidates and evaluating employees. One of our favorites is the DiSC Assessment, due to the accuracy of its data.

The DiSC gives you objective data on your candidates' personality and behavioral traits. You can use the test to make informed hiring decisions, select productive candidates, and promote smoother relationships in the workplace. The way someone scores can help you better understand how they handle conflict and honor your company's core values. Tensions can occur in the workplace, but you can build well-functioning teams with ease by analyzing the DiSC behavioral traits of employees who are involved in conflicts.

It also facilitates the employee performance review process. Many businesses use the DiSC test as an employee profiling approach to predict and monitor their performance. These tools offer a handy way to set performance benchmarks and motivate and encourage employees to achieve significant goals.

DiSC hiring tools are great for hiring employees in each department. By evaluating candidates, you can target specific applicants who have the right DiSC profile for your organization and are likely to meet their goals with much less effort.

Personality Assessments Are Not Biased Hiring

Equal Opportunity Employment laws prohibit discrimination and promote fairness and equality in the workplace. When hiring, you cannot discriminate based on factors like race, age, religion, gender, sexual orientation, or disability. Personality assessments are not discriminatory. They are unbiased, standardized tools that show a candidate's traits, skills, and suitability for a role. They can help employers match potential hires with positions that fit their strengths and preferences, and create a well-balanced, diverse, and productive work environment.

HIRING: CHOOSING THE RIGHT PEOPLE

As we've said, to scale up your team, it takes getting super clear on the kind of people you're looking for. You must give thought to the skills, experience, and vibe you want each person to bring to the table.

During the interview, you want to keep things genuine and focus on what truly matters in that new hire. Plus, it's crucial to make every candidate feel like they've had a fair shot.

THE INTERVIEW PROCESS

Interviews are your chance to get real. That's why long interviews can be helpful, as can multiple interviews with several people on your team, to get a better idea if someone fits into your culture.

A vital part of the interview process is determining a candidate's competencies and if they align with your business's culture and strategy. You want to find people for your team who not only have specific skills but also the capacity to learn and grow and who are aligned with your company's values.

We always ask interview questions based on our core values. For example, one of our core values is optimism. We look at challenges as adventures and face them with creativity and positivity. One question we often ask in our interviews is "Tell me about a time when you were disappointed with your career, your job, or your boss." You can learn a lot about someone's attitude based on a question like that.

If one of your company's core values is grit, you could ask questions about a time when the candidate was faced with a challenge that took determination, perseverance, and drive. If someone can't give an example from their past, that would let you know they might not be a total culture fit.

It's important not to rush the hiring process. As the old saying goes, "Hire slow, fire fast." Take the time to attract a lot of applicants for a job and then invest hours interviewing the best candidates. It's worth the time, because you will save yourself thousands of hours and headaches that come with hiring the wrong person. Trust us. Been there, done that.

TRUE STORIES ABOUT OUR HIRING NIGHTMARES

Before we established our company's values and a clear system and process for hiring, we made just about every mistake in the book. We'll share a few here.

We once hired a woman we thought would take our events and podcasts to the next level. It turned out she was putting on her own events and shows, with links to these events posted at the bottom of her work emails. It turns out those shows made anything on OnlyFans look tame! We thought we were on track with this hire because we involved the whole company in the decision, and our little team of five took part in the interviews so we wouldn't make a mistake. But we failed to complete background checks or do enough internet and social media searches to find out about *all* the events she was doing.

We also had an employee submitting double the hours she worked because she was doing two jobs at the same time—editing the podcast and answering company phones. We kid you not. This happened when we were not in the office very often, so it was difficult to know when she was acting as a receptionist or an editor. We would just receive her invoices and pay them. This was the result of not having a supervisor to monitor her hours. When we finally restructured our org chart and put her under the marketing manager, he noticed the discrepancy and called her out on it. This is why it's so important to have each employee report to a manager.

We had two employees who were so jacked up on Adderall that they would work all weekend on projects we never assigned and bill us over-time on Monday. We should have had much clearer boundaries as to what was expected and what was not expected, especially after the first time they did it. Back then, we just chalked it up to them being entre-preneurial, which is one of our values. We didn't want to snuff out their fire. But now we know that any new ideas should be discussed during our quarterly planning sessions and agreed upon in advance by the group.

We had employees who got drunk at events and hit on customers. While it seems obvious now, at the time, we did not specifically outline event protocol in our onboarding documents. And then there was the underwriter who would reject deals we found—we later discovered he had taken them for himself. As soon as we found out, we let him go. This was probably the result of not enough oversight, as we were becoming a remote company at the time. Today, we would have more than one person looped into the conversation and on the broker's email thread.

After all this, we were scared to try again. That's when we decided we had to do something different.

A NEW WAY OF HIRING

We needed to learn a new way of hiring. We were determined to get the next one right. That's when we found Jill, who might have been the most unlikely candidate but turned out to be just the right one.

When we were still operating in person, we needed an office manager to run things while we were away. We had moved our family about six hours from our office to follow our daughter's acting dream in L.A. We were armed with a list of company values and determined to only hire someone who fit them to a T.

We used the hiring structure we're going to outline in the next sec-tion, and added a twist: We wanted a question that would totally throw off the person, so we could see if they fit our relaxed and playful culture and if they could think on their feet. At the end of somewhat normal interviews, Rich would ask with a very straight face "What is your spirit animal?" Most people stuttered and stressed out and couldn't think of anything. But then Jill walked in the door.

She had bicycled to our office in a dress—already a good sign, because our slogan is "Live life on your terms." Jill nailed the interview, but at the end, she really got us. She answered the spirit animal question immediately: "Oh, I'm a hummingbird, for sure. They are hard workers, and get the job done. They also bring happiness and, some say, good luck wherever they go. When you see one, it means your challenging times are over, and healing can begin."

Isn't this the person you'd want at your front desk? Jill is still with the company today and, sure enough, has brought joy to many of our members.

OVERVIEW OF THE HIRING PROCESS

This basic overview of the hiring process is one we have honed through the years. Use it to help you find your A-players.

1. Use structured interviews to ensure fairness and consistency, focusing on competencies and cultural fit. Ask each candidate the same set of questions and then add one or two unique questions based on their responses or background.
2. Establish clear criteria for hiring decisions based on job requirements and company values.
3. Build your company's reputation among potential employees by ensuring a positive experience through timely communication, feedback, and a streamlined process. This might be the first impression someone has of your company, so it helps to get it right.
4. Adhere to legal and ethical standards to promote fairness in the hiring process.
5. Have a little fun with it!

ONBOARDING: BRINGING ON THE RIGHT PEOPLE

Onboarding isn't just about paperwork; it's your chance to make new hires feel at home and set them up for success. This is about more than familiarizing them with job responsibilities—you're also integrating them into your company culture and ethos.

It's important to make people feel welcomed and celebrated at your company. If you get the onboarding process right, you create a new raving fan of your business who truly feels like part of the team. When people have that connection, you have a much better chance of keeping them for life. (Well, for many more years, at least.)

At RealWealth, we've designed the onboarding process to make sure everyone's on the same page from day one. We ensure each new team member is aligned with our values and fully equipped to contribute from the get-go. We want a place where everyone's excited to jump in and make things happen.

We've created a digitized and trackable onboarding process at Real-Wealth that shows us how someone is moving through their onboarding, based on their completion of each step of the process. We used to have a one-page printed onboarding document with checkboxes. That worked well (for a while) when we were a much smaller company. However, once we had more than ten employees, it became challenging to track the progress for each new hire because some slipped behind while others rushed through the one-page checklist.

We changed our system to reflect our growing business. Here's what we built.

ONBOARDING TO HELP YOU KEEP A-PLAYERS

1. Develop a comprehensive onboarding program that covers company policies, job expectations, culture, and necessary tools. Set up a 30/60/90 form that includes a plan for what will happen over the next thirty, sixty, and ninety days in terms of org chart review, team overview, role description, key projects, key metrics, etc. (See 30/60/90 New Hire Onboarding Plan in this chapter for the program we use at RealWealth.)

2. Assign mentors or buddies to new hires for guidance and support, fostering a sense of belonging.

3. Implement regular check-ins and feedback sessions to address any concerns, and adjust the onboarding process as needed. Get those check-ins on the calendar so they actually happen.

4. Facilitate opportunities for new hires to interact and bond with their team members to accelerate integration. Onboard in cohort—help the new hire meet the other people they will be working with, either in a group setting or one-on-one.

5. Make it personal. Give or send the new hire a welcome box of gifts (company swag, a book or two, a bottle of wine, yummy treats, and maybe even something for a hobby they mentioned during their interview process).

REALWEALTH®

30/60/90 NEW HIRE ONBOARDING PLAN

Welcome to our company! We're excited to have you join us and are committed to making your first 90 days as enriching as possible. Here at our company, we strike a balance between professional responsibilities and personal life, particularly with our flexible remote work options that help you manage both seamlessly.

You'll find that our team is not only small and connected, but also filled with wonderful, caring colleagues who share the same intention of achieving excellence and fostering a positive culture. We believe in transparency, open communication, continuous improvement, grit, and collaboration to achieve our goals together.

We also offer an employee profit-sharing program to recognize and reward your contributions toward our success. Additionally, there are paid learning and development opportunities available to support both your personal and professional growth.

We understand the importance of rest and recreation, which is why we provide a generous amount of paid vacation time and holidays to ensure you have the time to recharge and enjoy life outside of work. We look forward to having you on board and contributing to our dynamic team!

In your first 30 days of employment at RealWealth, you'll be set up with:
- A RealWealth email address.
- A Basecamp account (for project management).
- A Ninety.io account (which runs our business operating system).
- Your own work phone number (if applicable).
- Your bio and headshot on our website.
- An introduction to the entire team/company.

In your first 30 days of employment at RealWealth, we expect you to:
- Learn how to use Google Workspace for your email and calendar (with help, if needed).
- Learn how to use Basecamp (with help).
- Learn how to use Ninety.io (with help).
- Review our Strategic Vision and Execution Plan (SVEP) in Ninety.io.
- Review our Accountability/Organizational Chart (with someone).
- Review the HQ Team Project in Basecamp.

- Review the complete RealWealth website and become a member.
- Review and follow all RealWealth social media accounts (@realwealth).
- Subscribe to our *Real Wealth Show* and the *Real Estate News for Investors* podcasts.
- Review the RealWealth Vacation/Holiday Schedule (we will provide this to you).
- Begin reading *What the Heck Is EOS* by Gino Wickman.
- Begin reading *Retire Rich with Rentals* by Kathy Fettke.
- Begin reading *The Wise Investor* by Rich Fettke.
- Get to know your team/department.
- Set up check-in meetings with your direct supervisor.
- Read the RealWealth Employee Handbook.
- Read our Company History, Policies, and Processes in Trainual.
- Read, understand, and memorize our ATOMIC core values.
- Learn how our employee profit-sharing plan works.

In your first 60 days of employment at RealWealth, we expect you to:
- Become more familiar with Google Workspace, email, and calendaring.
- Become familiar with Basecamp and be assigned to projects, etc.
- Become familiar with Ninety.io and learn how meetings are conducted.
- Become familiar with the Strategic Vision and Execution Plan (SVEP) in Ninety.io and know our company purpose, mission, vision, and goals.
- Become familiar with the Organizational Chart in Ninety.io and understand or update your job description/position/mission/roles and responsibilities.
- Become familiar with the HQ Team Project in Basecamp; rewatch one to two previous versions of State of the Company addresses, etc.
- Become a follower of and engage with all RealWealth social media accounts.
- Become a subscriber and engage with both *Real Wealth Show* and the *Real Estate News for Investors* on Apple Podcasts.
- Learn how to request paid time off (PTO), with help if needed.
- Finish reading *What the Heck Is EOS?* by Gino Wickman.
- Finish reading *Retire Rich with Rentals* by Kathy Fettke.
- Finish reading *The Wise Investor* by Rich Fettke.
- Complete your first few assignments with your team(s).
- Complete at least two check-in meetings with your direct supervisor.
- Read and start living our Core Values.
- Read and understand our Company History, Policies, and Processes in Trainual.

- Begin reading *Scaling Smart* by Rich and Kathy Fettke.

In your first 90 days of employment at RealWealth, we expect you to:
- Be able to use Google Workspace with ease for your email and calendar.
- Complete all tasks given to you by your direct supervisor.
- Familiarize yourself with Ninety.io to be able to create Issues and To-Dos, to take on Rocks (goals), and to be able to lead an L10 meeting (if applicable).
- Familiarize yourself with Basecamp to be able to create projects and tackle to-dos, etc.
- Familiarize yourself enough with the EOS system to feel completely comfortable talking about it with your team, etc. Note: We now use the RealWealth Operating System (RWOS), which is based on EOS but has been customized over the years to better fit our company.
- Familiarize yourself with the RealWealth website and engaged in content.
- Engage in content and comment on RealWealth social media postings.
- Watch previous recordings of the State of the Company address to be familiar with how we run and report our business data, results, wins, challenges, goals, etc.
- Become familiar enough with your department that your colleagues feel like you are a valuable part of the team.
- Set up and lead your department's weekly check-in meetings and/or individual meetings with those you directly supervise (if applicable).
- Have your first Quarterly Coaching Conversation with your direct supervisor.
- Complete all of your onboarding assignments in Trainual.
- Finish *Scaling Smart* by Rich and Kathy Fettke.
- Be an awesome example of our ATOMIC core values!

PEOPLE ARE YOUR MOST VALUABLE ASSET

Putting together your dream team is a mix of strategy, intuition, and a little bit of luck. It's about finding those gems who get what you're about and are ready to go the extra mile.

Remember, it's not just about hiring smart people; it's about finding those A-players who can take your company vision and run with it, making it their own. This is for you, the entrepreneur looking to scale your businesses through your most valuable asset: your people.

Being able to delegate tasks to your A-players is one thing, but real empowerment comes from trusting your team to nail it without micromanaging them. It's also about giving them the tools to grow and the space to kick butt in their own unique way. And yes, feedback is key—it's how you keep everyone moving in the right direction and feeling good about it.

In the next two chapters, we will do a deep dive into the delegating, training, and feedback loop with your team. Many people just hire someone and then expect them to figure out how their job works. The more clarity you have up front, the fewer problems that occur.

Here's to building a team that believes in your vision, brings their whole selves to the table, and is ready to change the world with you!

TAKEAWAYS

▶ You can have the best idea ever, but if you don't have the right team to execute on that idea, it will most likely die. A team of skilled specialists will help you achieve your ambitious goals.

▶ If you want to scale your team effectively, you need to find the right people for each position who will bring their experience, passion, and grit to your company.

▶ Before you begin to recruit for a position, get very clear on the outcome you want from that new hire.

▶ There are four components of effective recruiting: a clear job description, employer branding, diverse sourcing channels, and assessment tools.

▶ When you're hiring, find people for your team who not only have specific skills but also the capacity to learn and grow and who are aligned with your company's values.

▶ Take your time to find the right team members. Don't rush the hiring process.

▶ Onboarding isn't just about paperwork—it's your chance to make new hires feel at home and set them up for success. Yes, you're familiarizing them with job responsibilities, but you're also integrating them into your company culture and ethos.

- ▶ Make people feel welcomed and celebrated at your company. If you get the onboarding process right, you'll create a new raving fan of your business, who truly feels like part of the team.
- ▶ Using a digitized and trackable onboarding process is extremely helpful.
- ▶ Be open to adapting your processes based on feedback and changing business needs.

CHAPTER 9

LEADERSHIP FOR SELF-MANAGED TEAMS

Leadership is not about being in charge. It is about taking care of those in your charge.

—SIMON SINEK, AUTHOR

Building a team of A-players with unique strengths is an important start to developing a business that runs on autopilot. Next, you need that team to take charge, handle projects effectively, and contribute to the different areas of your business.

This is where the magic of having great leaders and self-managing teams comes into play. In this chapter, we'll explore how your company's leaders can create an environment where their teams thrive.

QUALITIES OF EFFECTIVE LEADERS

Leaders build relationships based on trust and aren't afraid to take risks to move the company forward. They also organize, solve problems, and keep a close eye on efficiency, productivity, and risk management, prioritizing the present and tangible outcomes.

Some leaders at your company should focus on the big picture—the company vision, innovating, and influencing your company culture. They're able to think strategically and assess how various actions will impact the long-term success of the team or organization. They set the direction and empower their teams. Your top-level leadership team will be supporting the other team leaders at your company to execute on the company vision and the annual and quarterly goals.

In a small business, the line between leadership and team management often blurs. The ability to switch between leading and managing, depending on the situation, is a valuable skill set. Be alert to this kind of versatility in your A-players.

The leaders in your organization need to be adept at talking to people, holding their teams accountable, keeping everyone motivated, and staying on track with results. They support day-to-day operations, oversee projects, and make sure everyone's in tune with your company's systems and processes (which we will cover in Chapter 12).

Effective leaders empower their team members by delegating responsibilities to the right people. This not only helps in better task management but also in the development of team members' skills and confidence. Good leaders trust others to make decisions and provide them with the necessary resources and support.

These talents, combined with a commitment to continuous personal and professional development, will create a solid framework for effective leadership. As Kathy's ancestor John Quincy Adams stated, "If your actions inspire others to dream more, learn more, do more, and become more, you are a leader."

Let's look at some practical ideas and inspiration for empowering your leaders to leverage their strengths effectively.

SUPPORTING YOUR LEADERS

In Chapter 7, we dove into the skills of being a leader of leaders and explained that supporting your leaders starts with your own humility, self-awareness, and presence. Those key qualities will help you inspire the leaders of your company to champion their teams to greatness.

As we mentioned, the performance of your leaders is a mirror of where you are lacking in skills or communication. For your team to execute effectively, make sure you're helping them to be the best they can be in their roles. That means clear communication, setting specific expectations, and giving direct feedback. You can also help support your leaders through ongoing education. Be willing to pay for learning resources, such as books, courses, and workshops.

Make sure to emphasize the value of using emotional intelligence. Leaders with high emotional intelligence can recognize their own emotions and those of others, allowing them to manage relationships more effectively. Emotional intelligence includes actively listening to others, paying attention to their nonverbal cues, and empathizing with their perspectives and emotions. It's also about handling difficult conversations with empathy or resolving conflicts peacefully. It involves reflecting on your own emotions, reactions, and behaviors and considering how these impact your relationships and work outcomes. It also means creating opportunities for open communication, where employees feel comfortable expressing themselves without fear of judgment. You may even want to provide workshops or training sessions on emotional intelligence to help your team develop these skills.

CREATING SELF-MANAGING TEAMS

Picture your business as a place where everyone on your team owns what they do and holds themselves accountable. This is what self-management is all about. It's a game-changing way of doing things, where everyone from the top down manages their own work, makes sure they're contributing to the team, and aligns with the big goals of the company.

Self-management starts with you and the people on your leadership team. The only way to create a self-managing team is to have self-managing leaders. Think of it as a domino effect: When your leaders get on board with self-management, they step back from micromanaging. This gives their leaders and even the newbies space to grow and make decisions on their own. We believe the whole idea of self-management should be part of your company's DNA from day one—every new hire should be welcomed into this culture from the moment they join, and you should be on the lookout for people who are naturally good at steering their own ship and owning their actions.

With this mindset, a leader's job changes from telling people what to do to being an inspiring guide to those people. Self-managing leaders set clear goals and point the way, leaning on the team's own wisdom to get there. Their focus is to make sure their team has what it needs to succeed, only jumping in to lend a hand when it's needed.

For team members, moving to self-management means taking personal ownership for their work, figuring out how to solve problems, and being part of important decisions. It's a chance to be creative and play a role in steering the company's future. When independence and autonomy are valued, it encourages people to play their part in making the business better.

To have a successful self-managed business, you'll need to be committed to creating a culture where everyone respects and empowers each other, holds each other accountable, and shares responsibility. These teams figure out their own game plan, goals, and how to get there, turning the usual boss role into more of a helping hand that supports growing independence and self-sufficiency.

Accountability is extremely important for team progress, especially today when more employees work remotely. One effective method is holding a weekly team check-in meeting to review goals, report on the current to-do list, and discuss action items for the week. Progress should be shared in a way that others can see that the work has been done to the group's satisfaction. If action items have not been completed, those items can be discussed to determine what needs to happen to get the job done and stay on target. During these meetings, new action items can be set up for the following week. This way, everyone is helping each other stay on track and honest. It's also a great way to discuss issues before they become problems.

Companies that make it through the change to self-management often end up with teams that are super motivated and truly invested in the company's success. The payoff can be huge!

KEEP YOUR MANAGEMENT STRUCTURE SIMPLE

In *Extreme Ownership: How U.S. Navy SEALs Lead and Win*, authors Jocko Willink and Leif Babin draw from their SEAL experiences to highlight how military leadership strategies can be effectively applied in business settings. A key topic in that book, decentralized leadership, advocates for empowering teams to function independently, minimizing the need for constant supervision. This quote from the book highlights the optimal size for teams and direct reports: "Human beings are generally not capable of managing more than six to ten people."

When creating a management structure, you want to keep it simple. It's much easier and more effective if you, as the boss, don't have too many people reporting directly to you. We agree that number should be six or seven people at the most. And if, in turn, they manage no more than seven people each, it'll be more efficient and a lot more fun too!

Imagine you've got six leaders who report to you, each with their own departments and teams. Their job is to inspire and support their leaders and their teams to keep the company's vision and main goals in the spotlight, not just for the year, but down to the quarter, month, or sometimes even the week. Your mission is to connect with your leaders regularly to discuss where the company is headed. Together, you'll be able to look at how things are progressing, figure out what's working and what needs attention, and create plans to get the most important goals accomplished.

Having inspired leaders help you run the show means you can trust them to support the team leaders and self-managed teams in your business, and make sure everyone's going in the same direction toward the same goals.

SUPPORTING YOUR TEAM LEADERS

How can you support your team leaders to learn, grow, and be more effective? Autonomy, balance, and accountability are all key.

ENCOURAGE AUTONOMY AND BALANCE

At RealWealth, someone recently applied for a position on our real estate syndication team. During her interview, when we asked why she was applying to work at our company, she said, "I really want to get away from the crappy culture at my current employer. They don't seem to trust us, and we barely have autonomy. One of the people on my team, who works from home, was actually warned not to take his dog out for a walk during work hours! The wild thing is that he is one of the most talented, hardworking people on my team. I mean, why can't they just trust him to do his job? He always delivers, but for some reason his manager wants to control his every move. I don't want to work in that type of environment."

Allowing team members to make decisions and figure things out independently, where it's appropriate, builds their confidence and develops problem-solving skills.

Leaders also need to recognize the importance of work–life balance. They should encourage their team to take time off as needed, use their vacation days, and maintain healthy boundaries between work and personal life. This kind of balance makes for better, more productive, more loyal, and happier employees.

AUTONOMY MEETS ACCOUNTABILITY

The most common fear we hear from business owners on giving their employees autonomy is "How do I know they are really working and getting stuff done?" That is an excellent question. You don't want anyone on your payroll who's not contributing at their best. Your employees also don't want to work with anyone who is not giving as much as they are.

So how do you inspire your team to operate at their best while still giving them the trust and freedom to work without someone always looking over their shoulder? How do you support your team leaders in accomplishing this balance with their teams?

Since we have been a fully remote company, for over twelve years now, we haven't been able to look over anyone's shoulder. Not that we would want to anyway—that just shows your team lack of trust and lack of empowerment. That said, we want to share what we've seen work effectively for motivating a team to take ownership of their roles and bring their best to the job.

The first step is to hire A-players, as we discussed in Chapter 8. You need to build a team of people who have unique strengths, do what they say they'll do, are bought in on the purpose and vision of your company, and get along well with their coworkers.

Once you have those people working for you and built connected teams, it really comes down to leadership and communication. Your leadership team is responsible for sharing the long-term vision and the most important goals from your planning meetings to their separate teams. Each team takes on those goals for their department or area of the business, moving your company toward the vision and the annual and quarterly goals.

The leader of each team then meets with their team to decide on the goals for each individual. For some, they might "own" one or two goals for the quarter or month that will contribute toward the completion of the big goals. Others on the team might have their own specific deliverables to achieve on a weekly basis. These are their key performance indicators (KPIs).

When each person on a team has clear deliverables, the team members (and the team's leader) are all aware of the results from each person on the team. This creates accountability, even when the people on the team have autonomy to do what they need to do to achieve their goals. Since everyone has "needle-mover" goals and KPIs and is checking in with the rest of the team on a regular basis (usually weekly), they don't want to let their team down. A-players welcome this type of group accountability.

If someone is consistently not on track with their goals or not hitting their KPIs, then the team leader can meet with them individually. (We'll dive into the how-to of that in the next chapter.) However, when people *are* hitting their numbers, there should be company acknowledgment of their success and performance.

Accountability helps create self-managing employees who form self-managing teams. It allows for autonomy and freedom without losing effectiveness and productivity. Since the team helps decide on each person's contribution ahead of time, everyone can trust that each individual is playing their part to help the entire team (and company) succeed.

One of the crucial factors here is consistent team meetings and clear reporting on progress, with goals and KPIs. When everyone has insight into each player on a team, it helps the whole team work in unison to create greatness.

KPIs

A key performance indicator (KPI) is essentially a type of measurement that helps businesses track how well they're doing in terms of reaching their goals. Think of it as a scorecard that shows whether you're winning the game of business. These indicators can vary widely depending on the industry and specific objectives of an organization. For example, a sales department might look at the number of calls made or sales numbers as KPIs, while a marketing department might track the number of new leads or sign-up rates. Essentially, KPIs give you a clear picture of performance and success in areas that matter most to the business and the team.

EFFECTIVE MEETINGS

Great leaders know how to run effective team meetings. This is an essential part of leadership, as it's how you connect with your whole team on a regular basis. But how can you know if you're being effective in your meetings?

We used to think we were having good meetings. Then we learned about how to have effective meetings from Jim Collins's amazing book *Beyond Entrepreneurship*. After that, we learned even more from Verne Harnish's books *Mastering the Rockefeller Habits* and *Scaling Up*. Then we both attended Dan Sullivan's Strategic Coach® program and began to incorporate some of those ideas into our team meetings. Our meetings were steadily getting better.

Then Rich read the book *Traction* back in 2014 and noticed that the author, Gino Wickman, had combined some of the best ideas from Jim Collins, Verne Harnish, and Dan Sullivan into what he called the Entrepreneurial Operating System® (EOS). One of our favorite ideas from the book was to have each person who attended a team meeting give their rating of how the meeting went. Wickman suggested that people rate the quality, effectiveness, and energy of the meeting as a combined score at the end of each meeting using a 0–10 scale. The goal is to have a Level 10 meeting (or an L10 meeting), based on Wickman's EOS.

We started using this approach and quickly learned why some people would rate a meeting a 6 while others might rate it a 9: Each person on your team has a different approach to communication. Each person on your team has a different capacity to speak up, be heard, challenge ideas, be creative, and so much more. By asking everyone after each meeting how they would rate it, we learned how to improve our meetings so everyone felt more engaged, focused, energized, heard, and happy.

We followed the EOS system for years and gained a lot of value from it. Then, over time, we began to customize the approach to create a business operating system (BOS) for our company that worked best for our business model and our team. Today we call that the RealWealth Operating System (RWOS) and it has served us incredibly well.

We highly recommend you read all the books just mentioned to help you design your own BOS, as well as learn powerful ways to hold effective meetings.

TIPS FOR A GOOD MEETING

Usually, the team leader facilitates the meeting. They keep an eye on the time and make sure the meeting format is followed and each section of the meeting is focused on the task at hand.

We start all our meetings with what we call "positive focus." Each person in the meeting shares one personal thing and one professional thing they feel positive, happy, or grateful about. This gets people in a better headspace, because when we're more positive, we're often more creative, we're better at communicating with others, and we don't bring a draining, negative energy to the rest of the meeting.

After each person shares their positive focus, the meeting moves into looking at the key numbers, the KPIs, and the results from the previous week and for the quarter.

Then there are reviews of each person's to-dos from the previous week and their quarterly goals to see if they are on track.

After that, we move into the most important topics, issues, and opportunities for the business. During those discussions, there are often to-dos and next steps created that different people in the meeting commit to handling in the coming week.

At the end of the meeting, everyone shares their rating of how well the team did with that meeting. Each person scores the quality of the meeting on a scale of 0 (couldn't get any worse) to a 10 (fantastic meeting on all counts).

That is a very basic look at how to structure an effective meeting.

COMMON TRAITS OF A BAD MEETING

Meetings are crucial for keeping teams on the same page, but often they don't quite hit the mark. Starting late is a common issue, and it sends a subtle message that time management isn't a priority, which can dampen the mood from the get-go. Then there's the challenge of staying on topic. It's easy for discussions to veer off on different tangents, leaving the main objectives hanging and unresolved. Lack of proper planning doesn't help either. Without a clear agenda, meetings can gloss over essential points due to time constraints.

Engagement is another stumbling block. Meetings that fail to involve the attendees or leave them feeling valued can lead to disinterest and unmotivation. Overloading sessions with too much information can also be counterproductive, turning what could have been an efficient meeting into a tedious one. Finally, aiming to cover too many objectives can scatter focus, resulting in little to no progress on any front.

For meetings to be truly effective, they need to start on time and foster an environment where everyone feels encouraged to contribute. Stay focused on the agenda while allowing for constructive discussions. By avoiding the common pitfalls of disorganization and disengagement, meetings can become productive spaces where important issues are addressed and resolved.

BE CAREFUL OF SQUIRRELS!

One of the most important things to know about effective meetings is that you need to constantly be on the lookout for tangents. This seems to be the biggest challenge when you get a group of people together. They begin to discuss one key issue, and then that issue reminds someone of something else that they then bring up. The conversation starts to go down a different path, and that reminds someone else of another topic, which they bring up. Suddenly, you realize the original issue is no longer being discussed because you've moved on to a different topic.

In our meetings, someone on the team will say "Squirrel!" to alert the team they've been distracted, just like a dog who sees a squirrel. It helps bring the conversation back to the original topic in a light, humorous way. If one of the ideas that came up during the tangent is important and needs to be discussed, write it down, so you can discuss it later with the group.

It often comes down to listening skills and managing your reaction to jump in and share your opinion too quickly. There's an old saying in sales that goes "You have two ears and one mouth; use them in that ratio." Many people don't realize that the easiest way to be a great conversationalist is by *not* talking. Have you ever heard people who seem to be reciting a monologue? They don't give you a chance to share your ideas or input as they go on and on about themselves. How do you feel when that happens?

When you talk, it is almost impossible to hear what the other person is saying. This is a common cause of both communication problems and lack of understanding. If you just take the time to *really* listen, you will see a major improvement in your conversations and your life. A simple way to remember this principle is the acronym WAIT:

Why

Am

I

Talking?

In managing, coaching, and partnering, having patient listening skills is fundamental. Rich used to have a little sign at his desk that said "WAIT." When he was in a meeting and found himself eager to give his opinion, he would glance at it and ask himself, *Why am I preventing this person from tapping into his or her own wisdom? Am I so sure about being right and giving the answer? Am I uncomfortable about giving them the space to be silent if they choose, which is often where the best answers are found?*

If you want to improve your meetings, your relationships, your partnerships, and your life, remember to WAIT. You'll be surprised at what you'll learn and the benefit that you, and the people you are communicating with, will receive. Make sure your leaders understand the value of this.

DON'T KILL THE IDEA PERSON, AND DON'T LET THE IDEA PERSON KILL YOU

The following scenario is an all-too-familiar one. A leader is holding a team meeting, having important conversations about KPIs, discussing progress on annual and quarterly goals, and dealing with any issues or challenges their team is currently dealing with. Then, someone starts throwing all their ideas out there about what else the company can do, how the company should do things differently, new ways to make more revenue, and on and on. The meeting gets totally derailed, and the whole team starts to feel the overwhelm of who and how these ideas might be implemented. All of a sudden, the goals that were set for the year or the quarter have taken a back seat to the idea person's brainstorm about what should happen next ... "next" sometimes being next week!

Don't get us wrong—we know that idea people are vital to growing a solid business, being leaders in your space, attracting new customers, and differentiating your business from those of your competitors. We need idea people! You don't want to kill the idea person's hopes, dreams, creativity, or drive. But you also don't want the idea person to kill your team's mojo. What should a leader do?

HOW TO HANDLE NEW IDEAS

When we're trying to grow our businesses, it's common for us entrepreneurs to have a ton of ideas swirling around. These ideas could potentially be game changers, but there's a catch: They need to be put into action!

When you get a spark of inspiration for your business, the next step is to figure out how to make it happen. However, you don't want to overwhelm your team with a barrage of ideas. If you (or someone on your team) is an idea machine, you've probably been guilty of bombarding your team with ideas before.

We call this the "buffet syndrome." Imagine going to an all-you-can-eat buffet and walking down the line, taking some of this and some of that. It all looks so good that you end up piling your plate high with a little bit of everything. It's like that when you overload your team with a bunch of ideas. You add so much "good stuff" that some potentially valuable and profitable ideas fall by the wayside, and you miss out on what can truly move your business forward.

To build something great, you've got to be selective. You need to take a close look at what's on your plate, so to speak, and pick the best bites for your business. That means saying no to some ideas or projects that might eat up your time and keep you from reaching your goals.

There are ways to say yes to new ideas though, without overwhelming your team or distracting them from the projects they are currently handling. We use a couple of tools for this, one of which we learned in the Strategic Coach program: the Impact Filter™. It's like a mental filter for your ideas and projects. It helps you figure out the benefits of an idea. Here's how it works:

1. You ask, "What's the purpose of this idea? What do we want to achieve?"
2. Dig deep and find out why it's important. What's the big difference it could make?
3. Envision your ideal outcome. What does success look like for this project?
4. List the criteria that will let you know if the project is a success.

Basically, you're giving your idea a thoughtful examination, and that's a great start. It gives you a logical basis to evaluate whether it's worth pursuing.

But wait, there's more. To really get into it emotionally, you've got to ask two more questions:

1. What's the worst thing that could happen if I don't do anything about this idea?
2. What's the best-case scenario if this idea is a huge success?

By answering these questions, you're not just making a rational case for the idea; you're also getting emotionally invested in it.

Many entrepreneurs in the Strategic Coach program use the Impact Filter™ often, sometimes even weekly. It's helpful for planning projects, figuring out how to work on them, deciding who will do what, and more.

Here's the challenge: The Impact Filter™ focuses mostly on the positive side of things. It's all about how an idea *could* work. However, we've learned the hard way that not every idea is a winner. Sometimes, we've been overly optimistic, thinking an idea would be a breeze to pull off or would only bring good things to our business.

That's where critical analysis comes in. When you critically analyze something, you're looking at the quality of the evidence and whether it supports your argument. It's a crucial skill in school, at work, and in life in general. "Critical analysis" or "critical evaluation" means:

- Connecting the dots between theory and data.
- Spotting relationships in the information.
- Giving your opinion and backing it up with evidence.

Don't worry—our next tool will help you do this kind of critical analysis.

BUSINESS OPPORTUNITY ANALYZER™ (BOA)

Critiquing doesn't mean just calling something "bad." It means weighing the pros and cons, appraising the value, and judging the worth of an idea.

That's where the Business Opportunity Analyzer™ (BOA) comes into play. It's your tool for critically analyzing an idea or project before you dive in headfirst. It can save you a ton of time and money by helping you avoid ideas that could turn out to be duds, or that might overwhelm your team if implemented immediately.

Here are the thirteen questions of the BOA. The next time you or someone on your team has a "great idea," put it through this critical analysis to thoroughly vet the idea.

BUSINESS OPPORTUNITY ANALYZER™ (BOA)

1. What is the opportunity or idea? (Provide a clear one-to three-sentence description.)
2. How will this benefit the company?
3. How could we create a simple sample or test for this idea (if possible)?
4. How much time would it take to fully implement this opportunity or idea?
5. How much will it cost to implement this opportunity?
6. Who would be the individual or team to "own" and implement this opportunity?
7. What is the potential revenue for this opportunity?
8. If this fails, what is the potential loss?

---

9. If it goes even better than expected, what is the potential gain, profit, or outcome?
10. How does this apply to our core business focus?
11. If this project or idea fails, what would we learn?
12. Has this opportunity been attempted before at our company?
13. If so, what happened?

ADDITIONAL QUESTIONS TO FURTHER ANALYZE THIS OPPORTUNITY:

- For the individual or team who would own this opportunity (Question 6), read the related job description(s), mission, roles, and responsibilities. Does this opportunity fit within the scope of the role(s)?
- What are the current priorities/annual goals of this person/team? Where does this opportunity fall among those other priorities? Should it take the place of one of them? Or should it wait until next quarter?
- What cross team/department support would this opportunity require (e.g., how many hours would we need the support of marketing to prepare, implement, and market this idea)?
- Who/what team do you anticipate might have an objection to this opportunity? What might be the reasoning for their objection? You may want to bring this idea to that person or team for their input before you decide to move forward.

When you have a promising idea, run it through the BOA before presenting it to your team. This not only helps you better articulate the idea, it also demonstrates that you've thought it through before saying, "Let's do this!" The BOA is especially beneficial for those "idea people" who frequently propose new initiatives without a solid implementation plan or whose ideas may distract from existing successful projects.

Think of it like this: If your idea can make it through the BOA—sort of like squeezing through the grip of a boa constrictor—and come out the other side looking good, then you've probably got something solid on your hands. This means it's been poked, prodded, and looked at from all sides, and it still seems like it will make your company better off. It's a great way to see if your idea is tough enough to stand up to the test and really make a difference.

When your idea gets some pushback, it might actually be a good sign; it's when things get tough that you really find out what your idea is made of. If it can stand up to the challenge, it might just be ready to take off. But if not, it may be time to let it go. Think of the BOA as the idea's trial by fire. You're figuring out if it has the legs to go the distance.

The Flywheel Concept for Effective Meetings

The concept of the business "flywheel," as detailed in the book *Good to Great*, by Jim Collins, serves as a powerful metaphor for the principle of concentrating on the core elements that drive a company's success. Collins asks the reader to imagine that they are tasked with spinning a giant, 5,000-pound metal disk. At first, it barely moves as they push, but with hours of steady effort, the disk completes a slow rotation. With persistent pushing, it starts turning faster, gaining momentum. Before they know it, what once felt like an immovable object spins rapidly with almost unstoppable force. The initial hard work pays off as each push builds on the last, creating a powerful momentum that makes the flywheel spin faster and faster, almost on its own.

The flywheel analogy illustrates how a business gains momentum: not through a singular, monumental effort, but through the persistent and consistent application of energy to the right activities. It emphasizes the importance of identifying and continuously nurturing the activities and strategies that have proven effective, while recognizing that pursuits outside of this core can distract and detract from the company's foundational strengths.

In the beginning, progress may seem slow, and the effort required may be significant. However, over time, the cumulative effect of these efforts leads to an acceleration of progress and growth. Each push on the flywheel represents actions aligned with what has historically made the business successful, reinforcing and amplifying those successes.

In contrast, the narrative warns against the temptation to chase after new, unproven initiatives or quick fixes that fall outside the established success factors of the business. Such distractions can scatter a team's focus and energy, undermining the steady build-up of momentum crucial for long-term success. This is exemplified through the failure of companies that frequently shifted directions in search of a breakthrough, ultimately entering a "doom loop" of inconsistency and underperformance.

The lesson here is clear: Sustainable growth and transformation in business come from a deep understanding of what works and a disciplined commitment to doing more of it. Anything that does not contribute directly to the flywheel's momentum risks pulling resources away from the core drivers of success, diluting efforts, and slowing progress. Businesses that stay focused on their flywheel, leveraging and building upon their proven strengths, set themselves up for continuous improvement and lasting greatness. This focus requires resisting the allure of the new and untested in favor of doubling down on what has been shown to work, ensuring that every effort contributes to the forward motion of the flywheel and, by extension, the company's ongoing success.

CREATING SUPERSTAR LEADERS

Helping your A-team become effective leaders is necessary to propel your business to new heights. It's your responsibility to support your leaders, so they can be superstars at their jobs.

If you're going to build a business that runs on autopilot, it's key to have teams that know what they're doing without someone having to watch over them all the time. This means creating and running self-managing teams. Your leaders need to keep everyone focused and productive while still providing autonomy through clear accountability.

In addition, you and your leaders need to run effective meetings that get results, and to vet all new business ideas that arise during these meetings.

Now you have the tools to do all of this!

In the next chapter, we'll discuss how to inspire and empower not only your leadership team but everyone in your company.

TAKEAWAYS

- ▶ Leaders need to possess many talents, from thinking strategically about the big picture to overseeing projects to motivating others. When these talents are combined with a commitment to continuous personal and professional development, you have a solid framework for effective leadership.
- ▶ Effective leaders empower their team members by delegating responsibilities to the right people.
- ▶ Self-managing teams are critical to your business running efficiently without your leaders having to micromanage everything.
- ▶ Your teams should have a mix of autonomy, balance, and accountability to do their best work in the most supportive environment.
- ▶ Keep the management structure simple. Ideally, no one should have more than six or seven reports.
- ▶ It's important for leaders to run effective meetings that stay on target. Beware of "squirrels" and use the strategies we outlined to handle things when the "idea people" chime in.
- ▶ Vet all new ideas using two filters: the Impact Filter™ and the BOA™.
- ▶ Remember the flywheel concept to stay focused on what matters most in your business.

CHAPTER 10
EMPOWERING AND INSPIRING YOUR A-TEAM

The most important thing is to try and inspire people so that they can be great in whatever they want to do.

—KOBE BRYANT, FORMER BASKETBALL PLAYER, LOS ANGELES LAKERS

In olden times, the definition of "inspire" was "to breathe or blow into or upon; to infuse (something, such as life) by breathing."[15] Breath is the essence of life. You can't live very long without it.

How can you inspire—help breathe more life into—your employees? What will light them up? What will make them want to show up every day to work with a smile on their face, eager to get started?

Antonyms of "inspire" include "discourage," "dishearten," "undermine," and "intimidate." While some bosses use these techniques to motivate, real leaders know those do not empower their teams. And yet, there are leaders who don't think they use those techniques—but their employees feel differently. These leaders believe they are inspiring their team members, when they are actually doing the opposite.

In this chapter, we're going to make sure you have the right tools to empower your employees and inspire everyone at your company, making them feel valued and happy about working there. We'll also talk about leading by example and the benefits of being a Multiplier (we'll explain later).

First, let's build a foundation of trust.

---

15 *Merriam-Webster Dictionary*, 11th ed., s.v. "inspire," https://www.merriam-webster.com/dictionary/inspire.

TRUST BUILDS EMPOWERMENT

Trust is essential for an empowered team. How do you build trust? Perhaps an easier place to start is to mention the things we know break trust: lies, deceit, cheating, stealing.

In our company, the boundaries around this are very clear. We do not tolerate any of these trust-breakers and will terminate any employee who does them. We cannot run a company with people who lie, cheat, or steal. That is made clear from the outset, as set forth in our core value of integrity.

There are more subtle ways that trust can be broken within a company and, more importantly, there are simple ways to build trust. The secret is to establish clear rules.

CLEAR VS. VAGUE RULES

Have you ever wanted to play a board game but didn't know the rules? It's not fun if you don't know how to play, and you might tune out or just put it back on the shelf. But when you do know the rules, then it becomes exciting. No matter how many times you play the same game, no matter if you win or lose, you want to play again.

A game is just a structure made up by someone who set a goal with some random rules. But when those rules are widely accepted, then the game gets enjoyable and competitive. People start strategizing how they can win the game. Not all strategies or skill sets are the same, but the goal remains the same, and that's what everyone shoots for. The winner takes great pride in being the best—even if there's no prize.

The word "rules" tends to have a negative connotation, reflecting rigidity and discipline. In reality, rules give freedom. If you're playing a game and don't have rules, how do you know how to play, how to win, or how to know if someone is cheating?

If your company were set up like a board game, would your team know the rules? Do they know what a "win" is? Are they clear on what is and is not allowed or acceptable in the game? Can they call out other teammates who are not playing by the rules? One of the best ways to destroy trust is to not have rules, or to have rules that are allowed to not be followed.

An example of this is when our daughter got her first job in the corporate world. She was so thrilled to be hired for a job she studied for in school: online marketing. She came to work excited, motivated, and full of ideas.

After a year on the job, the company increased their online sales tenfold. It was clear it was a direct result of her efforts. However, she never got a raise, even after asking several times and showing evidence that her work was a large reason for the sales increase. She later found out that her boss had taken credit for her work, and he got the raise instead. She went to the HR department to complain, but nothing changed.

Eventually, her motivation dissipated, and she started showing up to work like a robot—just there to get a paycheck and nothing more, like so many people do. Eventually, she quit and started her own online marketing business. All her inspiration came flooding back as she was able to collect income directly based on the ideas and actions she put into place.

Your A-players will not tolerate unfairness for long. They will eventually leave to play a more rewarding game elsewhere.

Are you sure the right people are getting the right credit in your company? Are you rewarding your employees fairly? Have you created a safe place for people to tell you what's really happening?

IF YOUR EMPLOYEES AREN'T GROWING, THEY'RE DYING

Life is never stagnant. Change is inevitable. That's good, because change helps us grow. A mentor of ours once said, "If you're not growing, you're dying." People need change.

As we mentioned in Chapter 2, we are teleological beings, meaning we need to be constantly striving toward a goal with a clear purpose. It's what has helped us evolve and survive as a species. It's not even the achievement of the goal that brings us fulfillment. It's the process of having a goal, figuring out how to attain it, and then going for it. The process of reaching for something that really matters to us is where we find our joy—it's deep in our DNA for survival.

It's our job as leaders to keep our employees growing, setting new goals, and working toward becoming the best versions of themselves. If your employees aren't growing, they are dying a little every day, and your company will die along with them.

You don't want to be the owner of a company where employees dread Mondays. Instead, what would make your team jump out of bed in the morning, excited to get to work?

LEARN WHAT INSPIRES YOUR TEAM MEMBERS

Getting to know what inspires your team members will help you understand and motivate them. Here are some simple, powerful questions that we ask.

- What do you want? I mean, what do you *really* want?
- How will your life be different when you have that?
- What *could* you do to have that?
- What *will* you do to have that?
- How will I know you've done that?
- If there was something that could hold you back from this, what would it be?
- Where do you feel tension in your body? If it could talk, what would it say?
- If you were lying to yourself, what might that lie be?
- If you were your own coach, what would you tell yourself?
- How can I best support you?
- How do you want to be rewarded for achieving this?
- How do you want to be "dinged" if you don't (for example, give money to an organization you don't believe in!).

These are the kinds of questions that can breathe life into your employees. If you want to inspire people, find out what inspires them. If you want to motivate them, find out what motivates them. If you want to empower people, find out what makes them powerful. Don't make the mistake of guessing. Use the answers to become a better leader to your team members.

BE FLEXIBLE

Can you stay flexible to keep a great employee inspired?

We did this with Maggie, one of our earliest employees. Though she was just out of college, with hardly any work experience, she was smart, organized, professional, friendly, and creative. Maggie ended up taking on live and virtual events from start to finish, organizing and responding to Kathy's emails, prioritizing tasks, and, most importantly, pulling the many ideas and thoughts out of Kathy's head that needed to be organized and implemented.

One day, Maggie casually mentioned that real estate wasn't really her passion. She studied art history in college and wanted to pursue it. Kathy was disappointed, as she felt she might inevitably lose someone who was perfect for the job. But she also had a firm belief that people are inspired when they follow their dreams. Otherwise, they go through life sleepwalking, which is reflected in their work. Kathy told Maggie that she was sad to lose her but happy she wanted to pursue her dreams. She asked her more about that dream.

Maggie said she wasn't ready to quit yet, but she was really into street art and wanted to create an app that helped other street-art enthusiasts find these hidden masterpieces.

"Sounds amazing," said Kathy. "I will support you in that however I can!"

Maggie asked if she could keep working at RealWealth while pursuing this other business on the side. That way she could build it up while still getting a paycheck. We said yes, as long as she kept up with her work.

Maggie went on to create an app that showcased street art in San Francisco, New York, and Paris. It was so successful, she was able to start a blog and interview artists she'd only dreamed of meeting. She ended up winning an award and receiving a grant, far surpassing what she ever thought she could do in the art world.

Then one day, Maggie told us she was ready to move on from her street-art side hustle because she had a new goal: marriage and travel. She asked if she could test out working for us while traveling. Her first trip would be to Cambodia. We said we'd be happy to give it a try—again, as long as she could keep up with her workload.

Maggie and her new husband spent the next five years traveling the world while also helping us grow our business.

We realize that not all companies can function remotely like this. But the point is, you can have "lit up" employees or depressed employees. By taking the time to find out what they really want, and then supporting them in that, you are helping them connect their brains with their hearts. And that's when the magic happens.

GIVE NEW RESPONSIBILITIES AND GOALS

Remember Jill, our employee with the hummingbird spirit animal? She rocked our front desk for years, greeting people by first name, giving hugs, and being the heart of our company as people walked into the office to get to know us better.

We had followed our dream to move south to Malibu, and Jill held the fort down in Northern California. She survived an office fire, saving equipment from the heat and some damage. She took the brunt of an angry homeowner when we made a too-low offer that was perceived as an insult. No matter what was thrown at her, she answered the phones daily with a smile.

But just as we had followed our dreams, Jill called one day and told us it was time for her to follow hers. She wanted to move closer to her family, so she could care for her aging grandmother, and would no longer be able to manage the office.

Kathy had a meeting with Jill to find out what was next for her and, specifically, what it was that she really wanted now. Jill said she had gotten bored working in the office. We had become more of a remote company, hiring people from across the country, so the office wasn't utilized as much. We ended up renting out some of the office space to other business owners, leaving Jill to manage them as well, which was not always pleasant since they didn't fit our culture.

Kathy asked, "If you could create your dream job, what would it be?"

"Well, I really want to pursue what I studied. Video editing."

"What?! We need an editor for the *Real Wealth Show* podcast!" Kathy exclaimed.

It was a perfect fit. Jill was able to move closer to her grandma while shifting her career into an area she wanted to work in.

As a result of this new inspiration, Jill took our podcast to the next level, getting it systematized, adding a video component, and editing it more professionally than we had. We ended up on numerous top podcast lists as a direct result of her efforts. She is still with us today, rockin' the podcast.

There are two important pieces of this story.

1. **People get bored.** They need goals and opportunities to better their lives. If you provide that, you will have happy, motivated employees. Believe it or not, working to make you successful and rich is probably not their number one motivation.
2. **People change.** What may have been the perfect position one year may not be the best fit the next. By staying in touch with the needs and desires of employees, you can move them to different positions within the company that foster challenge, growth, and happiness.

GAMIFY YOUR BUSINESS

Another way to inspire your team members and make them excited to come to work is to gamify your business.

Have you ever used the Duolingo app? It gamifies the process of learning a language. What used to feel like drudgery for most people trying to learn a language is a fun and competitive daily activity with Duolingo. Users compete with other users around the world. You earn points for playing, which elevates your status. If you don't play for a day or two, chances are you'll get knocked down a level and will have to work your way back up. You get extra points for being in the top three of your group, and you can share those extra points with friends and family who need a boost. Every day, you get to see your results and you get a notification if someone is about to take your place, which makes you want to play harder.

Our family has become addicted to this app. We all make sure we've each played one five-minute game before bed, so nobody loses points.

How can you gamify your business? What incentives can you create that get your team to be both supportive of others and competing to be the best? What daily rituals can you incorporate that keep people engaged? What metrics can you track that help people see if they are improving or not? And finally, how can you have more fun and make work feel like play?

CREATING YOUR GAMING PLAYBOOK

When you've figured out how to gamify your business, it's time to create a playbook. Here are the steps:

1. Make sure everyone knows what "winning" means. Define the end goal.
2. Have an easy-to-read guidebook that explains the rules of engagement.
3. Set up those bumpers (structures and processes) so your team can practice without experiencing a major failure for themselves or the company.
4. Hire a coach or coaches to help everyone improve their skills.
5. Celebrate wins often and lavishly.
6. Schedule regular one-on-one meetings for honest feedback.
7. Play more. Practice makes perfect.
8. Remember, it's a game. Have fun!
9. Lead by example. Be the best player you can be.
10. Keep recruiting A-players, so the rest of the team benefits.

PROFIT SHARING

Profit sharing is another powerful way to motivate your team, because when employees know they can get a share of the profits, it's like they become partial owners of the company. This makes them feel more connected to their work and the company's success. It's not just about the extra cash, though that's a big plus. It's about feeling recognized for their hard work and knowing that when they help the company do well, they'll see the benefits too. At our company we have a saying: "As RealWealth grows, your wealth grows."

This approach also encourages everyone to work together. Since we're all aiming to boost the company's profits, it naturally leads to better teamwork and less of the cutthroat competition that can sometimes happen at work. It's a win-win, because the company does better when employees are pulling in the same direction, and employees do better when the company's profits grow. Plus, it makes the company a more attractive place to work, which helps in keeping the good talent around and bringing in new talent.

We won't go into the how-tos of a profit sharing plan here. If you do some online research for "how to create a profit-sharing plan," you will find a ton of resources. There are also consultants who specialize in helping businesses do this. We hired a company to help us create our profit sharing plan many years ago, and it was one of the best investments we ever made.

Everyone at our company is part of our profit sharing plan because we are fully aware that everyone at our company helps us create those profits. We have clear revenue goals and profitability goals for the year and every quarter. Profit sharing both empowers and inspires our employees to perform at their best to reach those goals.

SUPPORT A GOOD CAUSE

As we've shown in this chapter, inspiring your employees can come in many forms, but one of the most meaningful is through giving back. When your company not only focuses on profits but also shares a piece of those profits with the world, it can be a game changer. We have seen that when employees know they're part of something bigger, their motivation skyrockets. They're not just working for a paycheck; they're also working to make a difference, both within the company and in the world.

There's something incredibly powerful about knowing that your hard work contributes to the bottom line *and* supports causes that matter. By choosing charities that resonate with your company's values and then sharing a percentage of your profits, you're building a culture of care and commitment. It's like everyone's job suddenly has this extra layer of meaning.

This vibe spreads through the office, making everyone feel more connected and driven. It turns the daily grind into something people can feel good about, motivating everyone to push a little harder, not just for the company, but for the impact they're making together.

LEAD BY EXAMPLE

One of the most powerful ways to inspire and motivate your team is to lead by example. Show them you are committed, passionate, and dedicated to your work. Your actions and work ethic should reflect the values and expectations you have for your team. When your team sees you setting a high standard, they are more likely to follow suit. You can do this by:

- Laying out your clear and compelling vision for the company's future.
- Sharing your company's mission with your team and helping them understand how their individual contributions support these broader goals.
- Acknowledging and rewarding achievements, both small and large.
- Providing opportunities for growth through training, mentorship, and skill development.

MULTIPLIER OR DIMINISHER?

In the book *Multipliers: How the Best Leaders Make Everyone Smarter,* author Liz Wiseman contrasts two leadership styles: those who drain intelligence from teams (Diminishers) and those who amplify it (Multipliers). Using research from over 150 leaders, Wiseman shows how Multipliers achieve better results with fewer resources, develop talent, and foster innovation.

A Multiplier is the type of leader who can scale their business and get it to run on autopilot because they empower their team members to be better leaders. Their job is to multiply the number of leaders in the company by investing in them.

Diminishers, on the other hand, are the know-it-alls. They believe they have the best ideas and don't want to hear the views or opinions of others. They just want their team to listen and follow orders. They don't care so much about the group learning or growing. As a result, their team members feel "stuck" or disempowered.

Which type of leader are you? Multiplier or Diminisher? If you truly want to create a self-managing business, then become a Multiplier. Rather than digging in too hard, working 24/7, and taking all the credit, look to the power of empowerment.

Here are some ways to empower your team as a Multiplier.

- **Spot and use people's talents:** Find out what people on your team are good at and what they love to do, then help them use those skills to the max. This might include sending them to conferences or higher-level classes to constantly improve their skills and knowledge. Maybe it means hiring a coach for them.

- **Challenge your team:** Help your team come up with goals they are excited and even nervous about. This gets them thinking hard and doing their best work. Think of it like setting a high bar but giving them a boost to get over it, with a big reward on the other side.

- **Give people the freedom to grow:** Be the boss who encourages, not the one who micromanages. Give your team tough tasks to stretch their skills, and then trust them to handle it. Be there as support, just like a coach would be for their team. If they fail, find out what they learned and how they can try again with a new awareness.

- **Encourage debates:** Get everyone to throw in their ideas and opinions. The best decisions usually come from a mix of different viewpoints. This works best when structured, because there are always louder and quieter people on a team. Maybe give a set amount of time for each person to share ideas and then a set amount of time for others to ask questions. You can also use the Tenth Man Rule, where you assign someone to be the dissenting voice responsible for providing a contrarian view. This will help the team avoid "group think."

- **Make everyone feel responsible:** Make sure everyone has "ownership" over some part of the company. This is about ensuring each person knows they're in charge of their success and mistakes, which really pushes them to be innovative. Each team member should have a metric or two that they "own" and take total accountability for, along with rewards and, potentially, consequences for the outcome. Each person should have someone they report this information to.

- **Lead with questions, not answers:** Instead of always giving out answers, ask your team questions. It gets them to think and solve problems on their own.
- **Challenge people to dream big:** Inspire your team and set high goals. Get them to see they can do more than they thought possible.
- **Learn from "oops" moments:** Make it okay to mess up and learn from it. Everyone grows more when they can make mistakes and figure out what to do better next time.

Being a Multiplier is about bringing out the best in your team, helping them to be smarter and do great things together. It's less about showing off your own smarts and more about making everyone around you shine.

Here are some bonus tips to take the spotlight off you and put it on them.

- Ask, "How would you handle this situation?" or "How would you do this?"
- Acknowledge someone's strengths (even better, do it publicly).
- Empower your team to ask for what they want, be willing to hear no, and then negotiate for a win-win.
- Be transparent and practice radical candor.

HAVE A CORE VALUE OF TRANSPARENCY

About fifteen years ago, we had our core values at RealWealth all figured out and even had them on a big colorful poster on the wall in our office conference room (back when we had an office). Everything seemed good. We thought all our employees were happy, that we had a solid culture, and everyone was friends. Oh, were we mistaken!

What we didn't realize was that some of our employees didn't feel heard, appreciated, or valued. Their managers were so focused on getting things done that they forgot to acknowledge the people doing things. We finally discovered this when one of our employees called to warn us that one of our best team members was thinking of quitting. This came as a complete shock to us!

I (Rich) asked if I had permission to get in touch with the disgruntled employee to ask how he was doing. Permission was granted, and the call was made. I said, "I was told that you might be frustrated with your job here. I care about you and want to know what's going on."

After listening to his frustration for about fifteen minutes, I finally said, "Well, let's take a look at how we can change those things so you can love your job here."

Once we had talked through a plan to make things better, our employee was deeply grateful for the call. I asked him why he hadn't brought these challenges up in previous conversations. He said he was worried that if he complained, it would create drama or frustration and that he might be fired. I assured him the only challenge that can't be solved is the challenge we don't know about. I thanked him for his candor and added, "I want you to know that you can always bring any challenge to me. We will find a solution. Even if it's a problem with me. I'd rather know than get blindsided." He agreed to communicate more in the future.

After that call, the leadership team decided it was time to revisit our core values. In that meeting, we added a new core value that remains today: transparency. Now, whenever a manager has one-on-one meetings with their team members, they review each of our six core values, and transparency is always explained and encouraged. Our managers let their team know how important transparency is to our company and to the health of our team. Everyone on our team knows that they can bring up anything, and we will seek to understand their challenge and look for a solution.

SET THEM UP FOR SUCCESS

Empowering and inspiring your team members is an ongoing process that requires dedication and effort. It can also be fun!

As we've discussed in this chapter, there are many ways to support people in doing their best work and feeling great about your company. You can lead by example, communicate a compelling vision, and foster a positive work environment. Be sure to recognize achievements, provide growth opportunities, and set clear expectations. Get creative with strategies like gamifying your business and giving profits to good causes.

When you trust and empower your employees, encourage creativity and innovation, and give feedback and support, you can create a motivated and engaged team that drives your company's success.

TAKEAWAYS

▶ Trust is necessary for an empowered team.

▶ Set clear rules for your business. Rules not only establish expectations but also give freedom.

▶ If your employees aren't growing, they're dying a little every day. Give them new responsibilities and goals, so they can become the best versions of themselves.

▶ Learning what inspires your team members will help you understand and motivate them. Ask questions to get to know people.

▶ Keep great employees happy by staying flexible with their changing needs.

▶ Try gamifying your business to make the workplace more fun, incentivizing, and engaging.

▶ Profit sharing helps everyone feel connected and personally invested in the company.

▶ Donating a percentage of the company proceeds to a good cause is a wonderful team motivator and a way to make a bigger difference in the world.

▶ Set a high bar by leading by example. Exhibit the qualities you'd like your team members to have.

▶ Become a Multiplier to empower your employees and lead your business toward being self-managed.

▶ Having a core value of transparency will help you learn when employees are unhappy, so you can step in and make sure they feel heard, appreciated, and valued.

CHAPTER 11
SCALING WITH POWERFUL PARTNERSHIPS

I'm no longer an artist, I'm a business partner.

—PITBULL, MUSICIAN/RAPPER

"Hi Kathy, I'm an avid listener of the *Real Wealth Show* and have been trying to reach you. I've got a deal I just have to tell you about!"

It was 2009 when I (Kathy) got this call. It was just another day for me, as there were "deals" everywhere. Big banks were foreclosing on millions of properties, builders were going bankrupt, and small banks were shutting their doors.

"Sure! I'd love to hear about it," I said, fully expecting another broker trying to sell me on a package of a thousand dilapidated foreclosures in the Rust Belt.

"I think before I tell you the details," the caller replied, "I'd like you to meet Fred, a local developer and colleague of mine. He's the only guy I know who can pull this off. He's been the 'go-to' guy for bank asset managers during every recession for the past forty years."

That piqued my curiosity, so I drove out to Carmel, California, the next day to meet this legend.

When I arrived at the beautiful multimillion-dollar mansion, an older man, probably in his seventies, was standing in front to greet me and my colleague. Fred walked us into his home and gave us a quick tour of the property—which, it turns out, he had designed and built himself.

We sat down in the garden by the pool for tea, and he said, "I've been retired for a few years but decided I couldn't sit on the sidelines watching all these once-in-a-lifetime deals go by." He laughed. "Besides, you can only play so much golf."

Fred explained that he had recently met with an asset manager at a large national bank. He had been escorted through the commercial division, where the aisles were lined with boxes piled to the ceiling, full of documents on foreclosed land, subdivisions, and commercial properties.

Fred told me he had noticed the address on one of the boxes. It was commercial land he had owned and sold for $6 million a few years earlier. Since he knew the property well, he made an offer that day for $350,000, and the asset manager accepted it.

He also was able to get in contract on twenty-seven foreclosed townhomes in Portland, Oregon, for $3 million, when the former value had been over $20 million. The homes were 70 percent complete and just needed the interiors finished out.

Banks aren't in the business of building or renovating homes; they just need to get foreclosures off their books. It was clear why the banks needed Fred … but why did Fred need me? I would soon learn the answer.

KATHY AND RICH'S TRIP TO OZ

Up until 2008, developers and builders could go to nearly any bank to get financing easily. But by 2009, few banks were lending, or even still standing. Deals were everywhere, but bank money had dried up. There had to be a different way to obtain the funding needed to acquire these opportunities. Partnership was the answer.

At that time, Kathy was transitioning from being a mortgage broker to setting up turnkey operations nationwide to help investors buy foreclosures, with teams in place to handle all the renovations and property management. Kathy still had a radio show on a large station in San Francisco, and Rich uploaded each recorded episode to Apple Podcasts. The *Real Wealth Show* audience was growing from locals in the San Francisco Bay Area to listeners in over twenty-seven countries.

Around the same time Kathy met Fred, she got a call from a woman in Australia who was a fan of the show. She had a large coaching program that helped her students build wealth through real estate. The woman asked if she could fly both of us to Sydney for a large event and teach her students how to buy foreclosures in the U.S. Of course, we said yes.

At the time, the Aussie dollar had doubled in value in relation to the U.S. dollar, while American housing prices had collapsed. Australians had the opportunity of a lifetime to buy U.S. real estate for a fraction of its former value.

When we arrived at the event in Sydney in January 2010, there were over a thousand Aussies eager to learn how to invest in American real estate. In fact, our office receptionist called in a panic because while we were in Sydney, some Australians were already in our California office, excited to buy property.

Kathy even had people following her into the bathroom at the event, asking if they could give her a few hundred thousand dollars to invest.

"Whoa, it doesn't work that way! I can't just take your cash," Kathy responded. "We need to find you the deal first."

And we knew just the right person back home to help us find those deals.

THE RIGHT PLACE AT THE RIGHT TIME

The timing was perfect. Fred had access to deals. RealWealth had access to investors. Soon, a partnership was formed.

We hired a U.S. Securities and Exchange Commission (SEC) attorney and started our first real estate syndication, with Fred as our partner. A syndication is one form of partnership in which limited partners (the LPs) invest passively, and the project is managed by the general partners (the GPs).

Through this syndication, we purchased those foreclosed townhomes in Portland, finished them out, and sold them for a big profit. Our investors ended up earning more than 22 percent internal rate of return amid the Great Recession!

There are many ways to set up a legal partnership. A syndication is often held within a limited liability company (LLC), but you can also form a corporation, an S corp, or limited partnership (LP).

While those are all ways to set up *legal* partnerships, we believe *business* partnerships can come in many forms. In the case of our Portland project, we created several types of partnerships that year.

- Some of the Australian investors partnered with us to benefit from our experience and connections in the U.S.
- Others invested passively, as it would have been far too difficult for them to buy foreclosed property and renovate it from overseas on their own.
- The real estate coach who flew us out to Australia partnered with us to grow her following *and* give her students what they wanted: access to U.S. property "on sale."

- The former owner of the Portland townhomes knew the property inside and out. He had lost everything when his bank failed and the construction loan disappeared mid-project, but he helped us get to the finish line faster in exchange for a piece of the profit.

We have done more than fourteen syndications with Fred since then, taking distressed properties and improving them to the benefit of our investors, as well as to the buyers of those properties who now call them "home."

We couldn't have done it without each other. We didn't have forty years' experience in development—and Fred didn't have a decade of experience in mortgages, broadcasting, or growing a massive group of qualified investors. A successful partnership often brings people together with vastly different talents, expertise, and backgrounds, all working toward the same goal.

Take Steve Jobs and Steve Wozniak, the cofounders of Apple. These guys were as different as night and day, but they respected each other's strengths and shared a dream. We'll discuss this awesome partnership in more detail later in the chapter.

If you want to scale your business rapidly, partnership may be one of the fastest ways to do it. It can give you access to new markets, resources, and expertise that might take you years to get otherwise. Bringing in a partner or partners who already have those skills is the ultimate leverage.

PARTNERSHIP ISN'T JUST BUSINESS—IT'S PERSONAL

Think of the best dating advice you've ever heard. It's probably related to communication, kindness, or honesty. Now apply that to business. Sounds odd, right? But it makes a ton of sense. Having open communication, being real with each other, sharing the same values, and gunning for the same goals are just as crucial in business as they are in love.

When you dive into a business partnership, you're starting a new relationship. You're combining the strengths, dreams, and know-how of a few folks in the hopes of hitting it big in the business world. It's a mix of excitement and "let's see how this goes." And just like any big move in life, it's important to weigh the good and the bad before you jump in.

Let's talk about the benefits of partnerships, what makes them tick, and how they can either make or break your business dreams.

THE PERKS OF TEAMING UP

Why partner with someone? Well, for starters, sharing the load means you might get to relax a little more. Plus, having a partner means you get to tap into someone else's brain—their experience and skills can fill in where you might be lacking. And let's not forget the moral support, better cash flow, and splitting those hefty business costs.

BUSINESS COLLABS CAN BE MAGICAL

When businesses join forces, some cool stuff can happen. For example, you can boost your brand's income: Microsoft and Zoom are big on this, thanks to their partnership. In some cases, these partnerships can even extend to co-branded marketing initiatives—such as how GoPro and Red Bull have established themselves as extreme sports lifestyle brands, working together to operate, film, and sponsor extreme sporting events in a way that appeals to an overlapping target audience. It's about finding those sweet spots where working together can open new doors and spark new ideas.

IT'S NOT ALWAYS A BED OF ROSES

Let's get real. Partnerships can have their downsides. Ever had a friend you just can't agree with? That can happen in business too. Then there's the whole sharing thing: profits, liabilities, decision-making. And if you ever want to sell your biz, or any of the assets you have acquired together, having a partner can complicate things.

Deciding if a partnership is your thing involves some serious thinking. If you've got gaps in your skills or resources, finding the right partner can be a game changer. But if the thought of sharing control or dealing with potential personality clashes gives you a headache, you might want to think twice.

TYPES OF BUSINESS PARTNERSHIPS

Here's a rundown of some of the different kinds of business partnerships you can create.

FINANCIAL PARTNERS

Getting a financial partner is the most obvious and commonly known way to scale. Simply put, the more money you have, the more assets you can acquire, the more people you can hire, and the more marketing you can afford. The following list includes some of the ways to get financial leverage.

- **Bank financing:** For real estate, this is the most obvious way to get money. You can more than 10x your real estate holdings by getting a mortgage. For example, you can buy an investment property that costs $100,000 with only $20,000 of your own money. If you're a first-time buyer with the intention of living in the property, you can put just 3 percent down! This is why we often refer to financing as leverage.

  Look at your bank as your financial partner. They want you to borrow money because that's how they make money. And they will keep giving you money as long as you keep paying them back.

  Successful business owners often have favorable relationships with their bankers. These are not normal mortgage transactions—they become relationships where the banks are trying to work with you to approve your deals because of your track record, especially the bigger your deals become. This means you may be able to get large credit lines when they don't even know in advance what you are buying. Community banks and smaller portfolio lenders usually have that kind of flexibility based on your past performance.

- **Government loans:** Small Business Administration (SBA) loans have helped many businesses get started and scale. SBA 7(a) loans are the most popular type of SBA loan. Business owners can get up to $5 million for capital needs: buying an existing business, refinancing debt, or purchasing new equipment. Interest rates range from a 2.75 percent to 4.75 percent (or more) prime rate. A credit score over 640 is required, along with a down payment equivalent to 10 percent of the total loan amount. In some cases, collateral may be required to secure a loan.

  An SBA Express loan will loan up to $350,000 with interest rates from a 4.5 percent to 6.5 percent (or more) prime rate. Generally, two years or more of business experience is required. While the SBA Express loan is easier to apply for, the amount of money you can borrow is significantly less than that of an SBA 7(a) loan.

  Look for participating SBA-approved banks, credit unions, and other lenders to get more details.

- **Private financing:** Private money generally has fewer restrictions than bank money, but it also tends to be more expensive. Many house flippers use private money to acquire properties that banks won't lend on, perhaps because the home has a nonfunctioning kitchen or other issues. Most real estate investors use private money for a short amount of time—to acquire the property and fix it so it meets bank lending standards—and then sell it as quickly as they can to get out of the high-cost loan.

However, there are some private lenders who want a longer-term loan and are willing to give a lower rate. For example, if a retiree is getting 4 percent in a ten-year treasury bond, perhaps they would prefer to get 6 percent interest from you instead for ten years (or longer). It's especially appealing if those funds are secured in first-lien position on a property, meaning the loan is recorded on public record in the chain of title. If the property sells, the title company would pay off the secured liens before title is transferred to anyone else. We know real estate investors who have built a multimillion-dollar real estate portfolio based on one connection with a wealthy person who preferred to have their funds invested in secured notes rather than in the stock market.

- **Private equity financing:** A private equity group provides money in exchange for ownership interest in your company. Private equity funding is not treated as a loan, so generally you don't have to make payments. Instead, the group acts as a partner and gets a share of profits. This can be a lower-risk way to get financing, but it may require giving up some control, and it definitely requires giving up a percentage of ownership. On the flip side, private equity can help you scale rapidly, especially if your private equity partner comes in with more than just money. If they also have expertise in what you're doing, hold on for the ride! This is often how small tech start-ups become billion-dollar unicorns in a short amount of time.
- **Joint ventures:** Joint venture (JV) partnerships come in many forms. A simple definition of a JV is when two or more people or entities sign a contractual agreement to undertake a specific task. Sometimes all partners contribute equal funds, while in other cases, some partners contribute funds and others contribute time, materials, or expertise. All roles should be specifically outlined in a written JV agreement, ideally drafted by an attorney.

It's important to understand that, in any partnership, if one of the partners is only contributing cash and nothing else, they are considered a passive investor. Businesses are required to file with the Securities and Exchange Commission when accepting passive investor funds. Always speak with an SEC attorney if you are considering using investor funds in your company.

Liabilities of Financial Partnerships

It's easy to think of the benefits of taking on financial partners, but it's critical to be aware of the risks.

A loan, for example, must be paid back whether your company is making money or not. If it's a recourse loan and you can't pay it back, the lender can go after your other assets to get paid. You can grow your company quickly with financial leverage, but you can kill it almost as quickly if you are unable to pay the debt back. This is why it's wise to take on debt cautiously and to be sure that whatever the funds are used for has the ability to generate enough cash flow to pay back the loan.

Take equity partnership as another example. When you have an equity partner, the partner takes part of the profit and may have some voting power. Just like it sounds, if you've got preferred equity, you're in line to get paid before people with common equity. Basically, this means you've got a little more security compared to someone with a common equity stake. But don't forget, how safe your investment is depends a lot on the property itself and the team running the show.

A preferred equity partner takes priority when profits are paid out. If the project is delayed or ends up having higher expenses than expected, there may be no profits left for the common equity after the preferred partner has been paid their agreed-upon amount.

Bottom line: Make sure you clearly understand the terms of your financial partnership and how the money flows—both the operating cash flow and the profits.

MARKETING PARTNERS

No matter how fantastic a product or service is, it won't sell if no one knows about it. There are more ways to get your message out there with marketing partnerships than ever before.

- **Other businesses:** Partnering with other established companies to help market your business can give you access to their customer base. This is extremely helpful if you're trying to expand into a new geographic region or target a different customer type. This is why mortgage brokers will often put on educational events for Realtors and their clients, or why pharmaceutical companies will give lavish gifts to doctors.

- **Influencers:** If you want your product out there, partner with people who have a large audience. You can pay a sponsorship fee for them to promote you, or you can try to get them to be raving fans of your product, so they'll share enthusiastically on their own. You can also offer them profit sharing or affiliate fees if they promote for you. Companies sometimes host events and invite influencers in hopes they will attend and post details on their social media accounts. Having partnerships with influencers is one of the fastest ways to scale up.

Become an Influencer

There's never been a better time in history for an unknown person to become a celebrity as quickly and inexpensively as they can today. You can create a podcast or YouTube channel with very low start-up costs. You can build a following on X (formerly Twitter), Facebook, TikTok, Instagram, or any other popular social media platform. If you can deliver engaging, entertaining, or educational content, you can blow up overnight. And if you do, not only will you see your business soar, but you can also create a brand-new business. Just ask the D'Amelio sisters, who posted some dance and lip-sync videos to TikTok from their home in Connecticut in 2019. A couple years later, they had amassed $70 million in earnings! If you don't have that kind of star power, resort to the paragraph above and work with someone who does.

RESOURCE PARTNERS

You can scale faster by sharing costs with other businesses. This can significantly reduce your operational expenses and increase efficiency. Sharing resources may also help you take on larger projects, conduct joint research, or fulfill bigger orders without the added expense. You might share facilities, technology, equipment, or staff. Collaborating with other businesses can give you access to a wider pool of talent by tapping into the expertise of their team.

I (Kathy) mentioned earlier in the book that when I owned a talent agency, I teamed up with the largest casting director in the area. I was able to use his space for free for my acting classes and utilize all his camera equipment; I even brought him in to teach classes at no cost to me. In trade, his talent pool grew, making his company more valuable.

STRATEGIC ALLIANCES

A strategic alliance is an arrangement between two companies that are not joined together in one entity. In fact, there is usually no equity participation in this type of partnership. The companies simply work together to help each other grow. An example of this kind of partnership is between Starbucks and Target. Their brands share a similar audience, which is why you'll see a Starbucks in nearly every Target store. Maybe all that caffeine makes customers happy and want to extend their shopping spree. Or maybe all that shopping requires a caffeine fix. Either way, the strategic partnership helps both brands.

BE CAREFUL OF BAD PARTNERSHIPS

An ill-suited partnership can be damaging to a business. A failed collaboration between Target and Neiman Marcus is an example of this. The two stores shared a clothing line in 2013. Sales were lackluster, probably because the two companies attract totally different audiences. Target is an affordable brand and Neiman Marcus is a luxury brand. Combining their two brands into one clothing design cut out regular Target customers who couldn't afford the new product and turned off Neiman Marcus customers who wouldn't normally shop at Target.

It's also important to remember that companies can take on the liability of their partners, whether they are legal partners or not.

The Australian coach who flew us out to Sydney to meet with her students is an example of this. She had been a busy accountant prior to being a coach, and she had decided to bring on a partner to help with her workload. A few years later, that partner said he was leaving the country and would be giving her the business back. Shortly after he left, an elderly couple showed up at her office with big smiles on their faces.

"We're ready!" they said.

"Ready for what?" she asked.

"For the return on our investment!"

It turns out her former partner had told this couple they could invest a few hundred thousand dollars into the company at a high interest rate. Those funds were now gone—out of the country along with the former partner—yet she was on the hook to pay the couple back.

Don't rush to enter a partnership. Think it through carefully before you get involved, and be sure to perform background checks and credit reports before signing on the dotted line.

A Great Partner Can Be the Apple of Your Eye

The story of how Steve Jobs and Steve Wozniak teamed up to create Apple is the stuff of legend in the world of business partnerships. They bumped into each other through someone they both knew and quickly dove into the emerging world of personal computers. They got a lot of their ideas and inspiration from the Homebrew Computer Club, a computer hobbyist group in Silicon Valley. Before they knew it, they were making this gadget called a "blue box" that let people make free long-distance calls. That was just a warm-up, though. In 1976, they really hit the big time with their first computer, the Apple I.

What made their partnership so special was how different the two men were. Jobs was the guy with the grand vision and a knack for selling, while Wozniak was the wizard with electronics. Together, they were unstoppable.

Despite what you might have seen in the media and documentaries, their partnership wasn't all about drama and clashing egos. Wozniak set the record straight in a chat with the *Milwaukee Business Journal,* in 2014. He said he and Jobs never fought or argued, and they were always good friends.[16] It just goes to show that sometimes it's that mix of different talents and a solid friendship that can really make a business partnership soar.

LAYING DOWN THE GROUND RULES

Before you jump into a partnership, get your ducks in a row. Who's doing what? How will decisions be made? Ironing out these details upfront can save a ton of trouble down the line.

Before starting a legal partnership, be sure to:
- ❏ Clearly define the type of partnership (GP, LP, LLP).
- ❏ Outline each partner's initial financial contribution.
- ❏ Define each partner's ownership interest in the company.
- ❏ Detail each partner's specific roles and responsibilities.

---

16 Alison Bautner, "One-on0one with 'Woz': Steve Wozniak talks Steve Jobs," *The Milwaukee Business Journal,* June 27, 2014, https://www.bizjournals.com/milwaukee/blog/2014/06/one-on-one-with-woz-steve-wozniak-talks-steve-jobs.html.

- ❏ Decide who has voting rights.
- ❏ Determine who has authority to make day-to-day decisions.
- ❏ Specify how each dollar will be spent.
- ❏ Clarify how profits and losses will be allocated.
- ❏ Define the process for resolving disputes.
- ❏ Outline how ownership stakes may change over time (e.g., through additional investments or transfers).
- ❏ Detail what expenses will be paid by the company.
- ❏ Outline the circumstances under which the partnership can be dissolved or terminated.
- ❏ Include buyout provisions in case a partner wants to exit.
- ❏ Address the process for transferring ownership, either for sale or in the case of death.
- ❏ Consider noncompete or confidentiality clauses.
- ❏ Consult with a tax advisor to understand tax implications.
- ❏ Discuss insurance and liability protections, including indemnification clauses.
- ❏ Have an attorney draft and/or review the partnership agreement.

RICH'S STORY: HOW I BUILT MY FIRST PARTNERSHIP

Back in the '80s, when I (Rich), was gearing up for the Mr. Massachusetts bodybuilding contest, I was a regular at Universe Gym in Salem. I was pretty much the walking billboard for the place, always rocking this satin jacket with the gym's name in big letters across my back. And my red Pontiac Firebird had one sticker on it: Universe Gym. Every time I entered a bodybuilding contest, I'd make sure they announced "Our next competitor is Rich Fettke. He trains at Universe Gym in Salem."

Money was tight back then. My job at an electronics store wasn't exactly a gold mine, so when it was time to renew my gym membership, I thought, why not ask Universe Gym to sponsor me? I wasn't asking for cash or gear, just a free membership. But the gym's owner shut me down: "No. We don't give away free memberships." I tried to reason with him, saying I'd brought them plenty of new members. Still, he said, "We don't give away free memberships. You'll have to pay, just like everyone else." I walked out of there feeling let down, hurt, and kind of angry.

I hit up other gyms, looking for deals like a free week or half off for a month. As I bounced around gyms in eastern Massachusetts, I noticed each had some great features, like loads of free weights, awesome cardio machines, a snack bar, you name it. But none had the whole package.

One day, chatting with my training buddy Scott on the ride home, I said, "I bet we could open an awesome gym that combines all the best of these gyms."

Scott was instantly on board. "Absolutely. That would be awesome. But we don't have the money to do that."

I was already hooked on the idea, so I teamed up with an older friend who knew business inside and out to create a business plan. We pinpointed the perfect location, determined our target market, and planned the features that would set our gym apart. We worked out the costs and cash flow for the first five years.

Showing it to Scott, I asked, "Do you want to partner on this?" He was blown away, but still worried about funds. "We still don't have the money to do it."

I decided to sell my Firebird and asked my parents to back me up with a loan. At first, my dad said no. I then told my gym idea to my mom, passionately explaining my vision and assuring her that I'd do whatever it took to make the loan payments—even if it meant taking on two full-time jobs should the gym not generate enough revenue or if the plan didn't work out. She asked, "If we cosign with you, will you promise to continue with your college education and get a four-year degree?" To me, that sounded like a yes! I eagerly promised her I would. Thankfully, my mom had a heartfelt conversation with my dad and managed to turn his no into a yes.

Scott had a tougher time. His mom said no, but his older brothers, who ran a vending business, said yes.

Even then, we were short on start-up cash, so we brought in another gym pal Brad. His folks were willing to sign for a loan, and that was our final piece of the puzzle.

In June 1988, we were stoked to open World Gym in Beverly, Massachusetts. It was a hit, growing from 8,000 to 23,000 square feet in a few short years. We added a retail store, an aerobics studio, and more. Our team expanded to twenty-four employees.

Starting World Gym and making my dream come true was something I could never have done without partnering with Scott and Brad. I picked up a ton of skills along the way, like how to manage a business, market it, handle the finances, understand legal stuff, and be a leader. Plus, I kept my promise to my mom and got that business management degree, with a special focus on entrepreneurship. Our gym business was a game changer for me, boosting my confidence way more than any degree could. I also figured out a lot about making partnerships work, and I'm still sharing those insights after thirty years, like here in this book.

Eventually, I sold my stake in the business to chase another dream of moving to California. But I'll always remember that it was teaming up with others that turned that dream into something real.

GET IT ALL IN WRITING

One of the biggest lessons I (Rich) learned while running the gym business came from my then-girlfriend's dad. He was a lawyer and helped us set up our business partnership. While he was drafting that agreement, he gave me a piece of advice I'll never forget and have since passed on to a lot of other people: "You need to spell out everything in your partnership agreement, and I mean *everything*. You need to define your roles; what would happen to the business if one of you died, God forbid; what needs to happen if one of you wants to sell the business; … everything." And then he told me something really important: "Written agreements prevent disagreements."

If you're thinking of going into a partnership, remember Jack's advice: Put everything down on paper. There's an old Chinese saying: "The palest ink is better than the best memory," and it's so true. We humans tend to forget the deals we make, especially when money and emotions are involved. Had we not had a written partnership agreement that spelled out exactly how a partner could exit, there is a good chance there would have been some drama when I wanted to leave the business. Instead, we three partners simply had to follow the agreement we had created seven years earlier.

I've seen business partnerships and even families fall apart because they didn't have clear written agreements, like a trust for inheritance issues.

Yes, partnerships can totally change the game for your dreams and goals. Just make sure to lay out everything clearly in writing before you dive into business together.

And don't put it off. I've talked to plenty of ex-partners who thought things would just sort themselves out, only to find out later that each had a different idea about their roles, money, or the business culture.

WORKING WITH A SPOUSE OR DOMESTIC PARTNER

There's another type of business partnership we haven't addressed yet: working with a spouse or domestic partner.

According to the Kauffman Foundation, around 70 percent of entrepreneurs are married.[17] So if that's you, there's a good chance you're working with your spouse or are at least business partners in your own household finances and investing. We would like to share our favorite lessons (some learned the hard way!) from our almost thirty years as a couple who run a household together, invest together, run a business together, and sometimes host business retreats for couples together.

We hope these lessons help you more effectively navigate the benefits and potential challenges of working with possibly the most important partner in your life.

HAVE A CLEAR, COMPELLING SHARED VISION

Many couples have not taken the time to discuss and clarify what they want their future together to look like. When we host couples' business retreats, that is one of the first activities we ask partners to do.

Each person writes down what they see for themselves ten to twenty years in the future if everything were to turn out just right. They write down everything they want in the major areas of their lives: family, career, finances, travel, health, fitness, romance, homes, assets, and more. Then, we ask them to share all of that with their partner. Most couples are surprised by how aligned they already are with their partner and are often surprised at what they didn't know about each other. After that, we ask each couple to combine their visions, wants, and goals into a single vision that details everything they want for their future.

Having a clear, compelling shared vision is exciting, inspiring, and motivating. It helps couples (and business partners) better know each other and become more aligned in the pursuit of that vision. We highly recommend this exercise for any couple investing together in those things that create more wealth, health, and happiness.

HAVE CLEAR ROLES BASED ON YOUR UNIQUE STRENGTHS

This is vital if you are business partners, and very helpful if you are simply household partners and/or parents. Don't share the same roles, especially in business. It can be a recipe for disaster, because you might think your way is the "right way," and your partner might think *their* way is the "right way." That can lead to conflict, stress, frustration, and disagreements.

---

17 Vivek Wadhwa et al., "Anatomy of an Entrepreneur: Family Background and Motivation," Kauffman Foundation Small Research Projects Research, July 8, 2009, https://www.kauffman.org/reports/the-anatomy-of-an-entrepreneur/.

Each of you brings a unique skill set and different strengths to your partnership. You are not the same, and you probably have seen that, in many ways, you are very different. That's a beautiful thing! Choose roles that are aligned with your unique skills, strengths, and desires. By doing so, you will both find more bliss in your chosen work, because it will be in alignment with what you do well and what you love to do. It will do the same for your partner.

A book that really helped us see the power of choosing roles based on strengths is *Rocket Fuel,* by Gino Wickman. Give it a read to help you get more clarity on what your individual roles should be in your business and your lives.

HAVE REGULAR CONNECTION MEETINGS

These are consistent weekly, biweekly, or monthly meetings focused on your business, financial, and/or other goals for the month, quarter, and year. You will be able to look at what's working and what needs your attention. You also will be able to solve any issues or problems with your combined genius, rather than feeling isolated and alone. Create a simple meeting structure and then improve it over time.

We recommend you begin with a quick check-in on how both of you are doing and what you are feeling positive about. Then, review your current goals and the progress you have made since your last meeting. Next, discuss any issues or challenges you could use input on. Finally, do some planning for the time from this meeting until your next one. What needs to happen? What are you going to handle, and what is your partner going to handle?

And that's about it. Keep it simple. These meetings only need to last about an hour to an hour and a half. Over time, you will realize the power of these consistent meetings to improve your connection and your understanding of what matters most to each of you, so you each can stay focused on those things. This will help you keep moving toward your goals and your compelling shared vision.

HAVE REGULAR DATE DAYS/NIGHTS

These are for love, romance, and connection … *not* business. Many couples who work together have told us that work conversations often creep their way into their time together as a couple. Have you ever been having a nice date and then one of you brings up a business idea or problem, and you find yourself in problem-solving mode rather than just enjoying each other and connecting heart-to-heart? We've definitely been guilty of this too!

To keep your partnership and your relationship healthy, there need to be times when you only focus on each other, without talking about business, finances, or professional goals. As a couple running a business (or a household) together, it is so important to have regular dates that don't include business talk. This is why having regular connection meetings is key. Those meetings allow you to create an environment to focus on business and goals, and you won't have to talk about them during your dates.

USE CURIOSITY OVER CONFLICT

This is simply the most powerful way to avoid fights, wounded egos, and disagreements. Rather than debating, trying to prove your point, or making the other person feel wrong, try being curious. We know this is a book about scaling a business, not about relationships. However, if you are in conflict with your partner, that will surely hold you back from scaling your business effectively and smoothly.

When you are fighting with your partner, it can suck the energy and the life out of you. By asking questions, being curious, and truly seeking to understand what your partner is saying or needs, you will avoid conflict and be more aligned 90 percent of the time. It takes presence, awareness, and an intention to ask questions rather than trying to be right or prove your point.

The next time things aren't going the way you want with your partner, be curious, seek to understand them, and maybe even say to them "Let me make sure I understand you. I believe that you are wanting _____ . Am I correct in my assumption? Am I missing anything? Do you think that I fully understand you?"

By truly listening to your partner and asking questions to fully understand them, your partner will feel heard and understood, and you will move through conflict with greater ease.

If your partner takes the same approach, that would be fantastic. They might not do that, so it's up to you to walk the talk, be curious, and really focus on understanding them. Your approach will most likely inspire them to act similarly over time—especially when they feel heard and understood by you.

PARTNER YOUR WAY TO SUCCESS

Partnerships can be a vital strategy for scaling your business. They can provide access to new markets, resources, expertise, and cost savings while sharing risk and promoting innovation. There are many ways to partner, all of which can help you leverage your resources and grow your business much faster with less effort and expense—as long as the partnership is based on shared values, goals, and a commitment to help each other grow.

Building strong and mutually beneficial partnerships can be a game changer for your business's growth and success. You just have to make sure you do them right.

TAKEAWAYS

- ▶ If you want to scale your business quickly, partnership may be one of the fastest ways to do it.
- ▶ A successful partnership brings together people with vastly different talents, expertise, and backgrounds, all working toward the same goal.
- ▶ Like personal relationships, business partnerships need trust, open communication, and a shared vision. They require work and the right fit to flourish.
- ▶ There are numerous types of business partnerships: financial (bank, government, private, JV, etc.), marketing, resource, strategic, and more.
- ▶ Partnerships can have their downsides. Disagreements can happen, and there will be a lot of sharing—from profits to liabilities to decision-making to selling the business.
- ▶ An ill-suited partnership can be damaging. Companies can take on the liability of their partners, whether they are legal partners or not.
- ▶ Put every detail about your partnership in writing, and don't delay. Written agreements prevent disagreements.
- ▶ Working with a spouse or domestic partner requires agreements, boundaries, and extra care.
- ▶ It's not just about getting together; it's about making the partnership *work*.

PART IV

LET'S GET NERDY (SCALING WITH SYSTEMS AND TECHNOLOGY)

CHAPTER 12

AUTOPILOT BUSINESS SYSTEMS

If you can't describe what you are doing as a process, you don't know what you are doing.

—W. EDWARDS DEMING, BUSINESS THEORIST, ECONOMIST, INDUSTRIAL ENGINEER

With both of us (Rich and Kathy) having more than thirty-five years of experience as entrepreneurs, we're confident that what we shared in Parts I, II, and III will make a big difference for you in growing your business with more energy, passion, focus, and grit. It will also help you attract those A-players who make all the difference in creating a self-managing business that continuously increases revenue, profit, and brand equity. And that means you won't lose your mind trying to get the not-so-motivated on board.

At the end of the day, we want to help entrepreneurs and business leaders build more *organized and efficient* businesses. We know how important it is to be able to run your business with a clear understanding of the measurables and processes that will allow you to take your company to the next level and beyond. That is what we will cover in Part IV of this book.

It's not about you working harder. It's about you working smarter. Rather than doing more, you have to find a way to do less but for your *business* to do more. How? By designing systems that are built from the individual processes in each area of your business.

Businesses need well-defined systems and processes to ensure consistency, efficiency, and scalability. Without them, a business can become chaotic and overwhelming, and it will struggle to achieve its goals. This chapter is about creating a practical framework for improving the way your company operates and scales, resulting in more ease and freedom for you and your team. Let's dig into the next phase of scaling your business!

First, all of you visionaries out there, take a few deep breaths. We are going to talk about processes and procedures now. You might want to tune out, but don't. You don't have to be the one who implements these systems and processes into your company, but you *do* need to know their importance.

For those analyst types whose patience may have been tested by all the "fluffy" purpose, mission, vision, and values stuff we've covered so far, you'll feel right at home digging into systems, processes, KPIs, and all the important left-brained aspects of scaling a business the smart way.

When we talk about "scaling smart," we're talking about ramping up your business to handle more customers, more sales, and more of whatever you're offering without dropping the ball on how well your company runs or how much profit you make. A big part of accomplishing this is setting up a *scalable infrastructure*—which means putting together systems and processes that can grow with your business. This is a huge step toward making your business run like a well-oiled machine—a business on autopilot.

YOUR BUSINESS ON AUTOPILOT—LIKE A TESLA

Have you ever been in a vehicle with self-driving capability? It's quite amazing to witness. We have both driven Teslas for several years, and we love the autopilot feature. It's like something straight out of a futuristic movie.

Guess what? Those autopilot principles can work wonders for your business too. Imagine running your business so smoothly it's like cruising down the highway in a Tesla with self-driving engaged.

Tesla's Autopilot AI team is focused on the future of autonomous driving. They're constantly tweaking and improving things—just like you should be doing with your business to scale it up and make things run like clockwork.

Teslas have eight cameras and some amazing vision processing that gives the car a 360-degree view. In your business, you can do something similar by using processes, systems, and data to provide insight into what's working and what needs improvement.

Tesla's "neural network" is the brain behind their Autopilot. For your business, it's all about designing scalable processes that explain how your business thinks and operates. Think of it as building the infrastructure that puts your business on autopilot mode.

Tesla's Navigate on Autopilot feature suggests lane changes to optimize the route, and even steers your car toward highway exits. In your business, having the right systems and processes allows your team to consistently optimize the path you take toward your company mission and vision.

But there's a catch: Tesla's Autopilot still needs a human in the driver's seat, and your business should keep that human touch too. Automation is cool, but you'll always need real people to make big decisions, come up with fresh ideas, and deal with customers.

Watching a Tesla on Autopilot is like seeing magic happen, and it's the same with your business. By scaling smart, setting up scalable systems and processes, and having the right team of people, you can steer your business into a future where it practically runs itself. This will allow you, the business owner, to simply glance at your dashboard and then the road ahead to ensure everything is going well and you are heading in the right direction. Putting your business on autopilot means trusting your team to run things effectively while you are continuously optimizing the systems and processes that will maximize your wealth and your freedom.

Your business can only grow to the level of your systems and processes.

—AJ OSBORNE, CEO, CEDAR CREEK CAPITAL

WHY ARE SYSTEMS AND PROCESSES SO IMPORTANT?

When I (Kathy) brought Rich on as my business partner, I didn't have many systems in place. I wasn't technologically savvy, so our business didn't have fancy software programs. Instead, we often handled details manually. I didn't know how to properly onboard and train people, so we didn't have an employee manual. People just had to figure things out—and they weren't always qualified to do so. We didn't track sales leads, so we were most certainly leaving money on the table. It's more like I was driving an old stick shift in need of constant repair than a Tesla on Autopilot! By automating our systems and processes, Rich helped us operate much more efficiently, leading us toward achieving our own autopilot mode, so we could scale the business.

Here's a small example of how having a digitized process in your business can help. Imagine that instead of digging through a pile of papers on your desk to find the one you need, you open your computer and, with one or two clicks, find what you're looking for. And it's just as accessible to everyone in the company who may need it. A ten-minute job turned into a thirty-second task.

Another example of process on a larger scale is Starbucks. Before their beloved coffee can make its way into our cups, it goes through quite a process of transformation—it actually starts off as seeds! Starbucks gets its hands on the raw stuff—coffee beans, which are seeds from the coffee tree. Once they've got the beans, they stash them away in storage. Before any roasting happens, there's a bit of housekeeping to do. The beans get sifted and sorted in a thorough, multistep process to make sure only the best make the cut.

Next up, roasting. Those unroasted beans, also known as green coffee, are full of untapped flavors. Roasting them is where the magic happens, changing their chemical and physical makeup. The beans are heated to over 400 degrees Fahrenheit and, depending on how long they're roasted, develop different characteristics and flavors.

Then comes the blending. This step is all about mixing those different roasted beans together to create signature Starbucks flavors. They use pneumatic conveyors to move the beans without exposing them to air, letting all the unwanted gases escape.

Packaging is crucial, because once coffee is exposed to air, it can clump up or lose its taste, especially the ground kind. The goal is to keep those beans safe from air and moisture, so they stay fresh. Once everything's sealed up tight, it's off to Starbucks stores.

But wait, there's more! Before you can enjoy your brew, those beans need to be ground up. Grinding, or milling, the coffee right before brewing makes sure you're getting the freshest flavor. The grind size varies depending on how you're making your coffee (drip, espresso, French roast, etc.).

Finally, it's brewing time. Getting the perfect cup depends on the brew temperature, grind size, and the coffee-to-water ratio.

And then, the best part of the process: drinking that coffee.

The next time you're sipping on a Starbucks creation, take a moment to appreciate all the effort that went into making it. Turns out, making great coffee involves clearly documented processes and a lot of expertise. Each step in the process has been tested and optimized over time. Plus, every step has been recorded into a digitized document to help guide each employee and team for consistency, efficiency, and continuous improvement.

What Good Processes Look Like

Tarl Yarber, whom we first mentioned in Chapter 2, is the entrepreneurial force behind Fixated Real Estate. With businesses that include property flipping, conferences on financial freedom and real estate, BRRRR investing, and more, Tarl is a champion of using systems for scaling. At Fixated Real Estate, Tarl's team has created processes for every part of their real estate acquisitions, rehabbing, selling, and holding.

One such process is an employee guide to packaging properties for purchase. It lists the required documentation, processes, and data needed to decide whether the company should buy a property. This memorandum spells out in great detail, step by step, what an employee needs to do—such as where the computer folder is located for storing the information, exactly how the information should be labeled, and what types of data and photos should be collected and stored in there for each potential property. This process helps Tarl's team make quick, informed decisions about purchases and creates uniformity in all the documentation.

Another process explains the steps of a successful initial property walk. This helps Tarl's team members collect data on and evaluate a prospective property for purchase: taking the appropriate photos and videos; seeking out and evaluating key rehab components; and doing a thorough walkthrough of the property, collecting all important information.

"The key to an effective system or process on my team is that it has to be clear, simple, accountable, and duplicatable," Tarl says. "And one of the most important parts—that it makes my life easier."

You need to both automate and streamline your business operations to reduce costs and improve efficiency. You should be looking for opportunities to eliminate bottlenecks, optimize workflows, and reduce manual tasks. Implementing systems and processes into your business helps make these goals possible.

Finally, if you aren't satisfied with all these reasons for having clear and repeatable systems and processes in place, maybe this will motivate you: The value of your business is directly correlated to the sophistication of your systems and processes. No one will be interested in buying a business where all the details are in *your* head. If you ever want to exit your business with lots of zeros in your buyout, it must be something that can operate just fine (or even better) without you in it. Otherwise, plan to be in it for the rest of your life.

PROCESSES VS. SYSTEMS: WHAT'S THE DIFFERENCE?

A business "process" is like a company's to-do list for getting stuff done. It's a bunch of organized tasks or activities that a company does to reach a specific goal. Usually, these tasks are all about improving their products or services, making things run smoother, and keeping customers happy.

Business processes can be simple or complicated, depending on what the business is and what it's trying to achieve. Your processes might include how you acquire new customers, perform sales, process orders, manage inventory, handle customer service, develop new products or services, and onboard new employees.

A series of business processes comprises a "system." A business system is like the behind-the-scenes magic that makes a company tick. It's basically a group of things—processes, procedures, functions—that work together to make sure the company reaches its goals. The system ensures that multiple operations work in sync and run efficiently in the world of business.

If we tried to detail all the steps to create and document your business systems and processes, it would double the size of this book. There are numerous how-to books, videos, and articles on this subject that will teach you (or your team) how to excel in this area. Just do a quick search online or at your favorite bookstore, and you'll see what we mean.

However, we want you to understand the importance of building systems and processes, so we'll do a basic overview here. Ready? Let's do this!

HOW TO CREATE PROCESSES

Whether your company has been around for a long time or your business is fairly new, you probably have a few processes you already follow. Getting them documented shouldn't take too much time. If you are the one following those processes, then it's best for you to carve out some time each week to document them, so they'll be ready for your next hire.

You'll also need to create some new processes. Creating a process is basically organizing and codifying a set of tasks that your company does to reach a goal—like making operations smoother, improving your products, or taking care of your customers or clients. These processes are sometimes simple, but they can end up being quite complex. It really depends on what steps are involved and what the goal is.

The most important parts of a business process include:

- **Purpose**—Each process has a goal to achieve a specific outcome.
- **Activities**—The tasks or the steps in the process, done in a certain order.
- **Inputs and outputs**—Every step uses resources (inputs) and produces something (outputs) toward your goal.
- **Workflow**—The order in which the tasks are done, which can change based on different situations.
- **Roles and responsibilities**—The people or groups who are responsible for each step in the process.
- **Automation**—How technology is used to make the process more efficient.
- **Metrics and key performance indicators (KPIs)** —Data used to measure and track your process's performance.
- **Continuous improvement**—A way to regularly update and refine the process to adapt to a new need or to improve performance.

Here are the steps of creating a process.

1. Write down a step-by-step list of one of the tasks you do repeatedly. (It will be more accurate if you *do* the work and document each step as you move through it.) If it's already automated through technology, list out how to access that technology (what software or app is used), including how to log in. Your processes might include:
   - Step-by-step instructions and checklists.
   - Contracts and agreements used with vendors and affiliates.
   - Sales scripts.
   - Customer service scripts.
   - Frequently asked questions (FAQs).
   - How you process and file paperwork and forms.
   - How you handle customer complaints or problems.
   - How to use different types of software and apps.
   - How to access and use your company's customer relationship software (CRM).
   - How to create and use marketing and customer service follow-up campaigns.
   - How you run meetings.

- How you use data to analyze and predict the health of your business.
- How you track KPIs for people and departments.
- Anything else you can think of for your unique business model.

2. Once you have finished writing down each step of the process, go back and imagine you are someone who has no idea how to do that process. Then go through the process and ensure that you have covered every possible step and question that someone would have. Better yet, ask someone who doesn't know much about your job to do the process as you observe what works and what needs further explanation to complete the process correctly and effectively.

By getting all those steps, checklists, and pieces of information out of your brain (or the brain of another person on your team) and into a document, you not only create a well-oiled business machine, you also avoid the emergencies, stress, and drama that would happen if someone leaves the company without sharing the system with others. Think about your business. What would happen if you lost one of your key people tomorrow? Would someone else be able to step into their position and handle things effectively? What if you wanted to or had to step away from your business for thirty days? Would your business continue to run smoothly and without a hiccup?

If this all sounds overwhelming to you, then we have just identified your next hire! Just like authors hire ghostwriters who can pull out the key points from the author's message and put those ideas into a readable and digestible award-winning book (don't think we didn't do that!), there are people out there who absolutely love to create systems—it's their superpower. Let them pull from you the key things that you do, and then let them create the systems for you.

Well-run business processes are crucial for your company's success. In addition to the benefits we already mentioned, they will lead to cost savings, better quality, and happier customers and clients.

KATHY'S STORY

When I (Kathy) first started the *Real Wealth Show* podcast, back in 2005, I didn't have any written processes or systems (by now this shouldn't surprise you). I just interviewed whomever I wanted, didn't have a set list of questions to ask my guests, and had no time limit for the interview. Most of the time, I would just show up at the studio and talk from my heart. In other words, there was a lot of rambling. I was also very inconsistent with show releases. Sometimes I would do two or three shows per week, and other times I'd go months without doing one!

While we did have a good following nonetheless (thank you to my loyal listeners who had no idea when I'd release a new podcast!), things really took off when we started building systems and processes for the show. And what I mean by "we" is that Rich and I put one of our employees in charge as the bottom-line person to make sure we stayed on schedule. We both knew I'd get too busy or distracted to be held accountable to a set schedule.

We set a day for the weekly release, a length for each show of about twenty minutes, and a process for the guest to follow, with a questionnaire sent to them in advance. This new process improved the content, grew the listenership, and kept the show in the top ten real estate podcasts for many years.

More importantly, I discovered that, as a very strong visionary and weak structures and systems person, I needed my support team to have qualities opposite of mine. They set up the structures and processes so that all I had to do was follow them. This took an enormous amount of stress off me and saved hours of time, because everything I ever needed was in one easy-to-find organizational software program (more on this software later in the chapter).

Big-Idea People, Take Note

People who start businesses are not always the same people who keep businesses thriving. Business starters are often just that: They have big ideas and the ability to get them off the ground. However, they often get bored with the day-to-day operations required to keep the company running smoothly and effectively in the long run. Instead, they're ready to start a new business or move the current business in a different direction, which can be risky. All those ideas and changes can also burn out their employees.

Once a business is off the ground and showing success in the marketplace, it's time to create systems and processes. And it may be time for the business starter to hand over the reins to the "slow and steady" employees. In Kathy's case, this meant she almost had to become an employee of her employees. In other words, she asked them to hold her accountable to following the systems and processes they had put in place. She asked them to treat her like anyone else who might derail a meeting or try to present a new idea without the proper procedure in place.

It takes humility to allow your team to run things, but it's the only way to grow leaders within the company so that it can eventually run on autopilot.

If you are the big-idea person, you may be used to calling the shots. Submitting to systems your team has put in place may feel like it's killing your spirit, but we assure you, if you don't, you will kill your company.

We know that might sound like a lot of work! However, while documenting processes can be a pain for visionary types and it can be hard for them to "find the time," it's worth it because it actually *frees up their time* in the future to do what they do best. Proper documentation is not a days-long or even weeks-long task, but it will save you that amount of time (and more!) down the road. The payoff is huge.

We have seen far too many times when a big-idea person ignored the wisdom of their team. You hired your bookkeeper, your operations team, and maybe your business coach for a reason. Listen to them carefully before making decisions. Better yet, let them be part of the decision-making, because at the end of the day, they will be the ones carrying out the idea.

However, it is important to stay relevant and keep evolving. This is the job of the big-idea person. That's why large companies often have research and development (R&D) divisions. These are separate teams or even different companies where new ideas can be tested. These ideas should have their own business plan before launching, showing exactly what expenses are projected versus income. Since the business that's making money shouldn't be derailed by new ideas, and the current staff is probably already maxed, a new team needs to be hired for the R&D division. That division should really be treated like a start-up, because essentially it is. We don't want the visionary spirit to ever die.

Systems run the business and people run the systems.

—MICHAEL GERBER, AUTHOR, *THE E-MYTH REVISITED: WHY MOST SMALL BUSINESSES FAIL AND WHAT TO DO ABOUT IT*

HAVE YOUR TEAM CREATE THEIR OWN PROCESSES

If you want to put your business on autopilot, you need a great team of people who use systems and processes effectively and consistently. But don't get stuck thinking about how much time and effort it's going to take you to create all the systems and processes in your business.

A more effective approach that will free up some of your time and energy is to ask the person who is following a certain process to document that process. That person should be the one responsible for that key outcome for the company—and their job description should include the top four to seven roles and responsibilities.

For example, a real estate broker might have the following roles and responsibilities.

- Listing homes for sale, usually on the Multiple Listing Service (MLS)
- Supervising property showings
- Reporting results and feedback of a sale to the sellers
- Helping buyers locate properties within their desired geographical area
- Assisting buyers with visiting properties
- Working with buyers during the sale

These roles and responsibilities should all have clearly documented processes. This way, if that person ever leaves your company, your team won't be left in confusion or overwhelm about how to step in and handle those responsibilities. And if you do hire a replacement, they will have an already documented process to simplify their onboarding and can get into the flow much faster and easier than trying to figure out everything from scratch. If possible, make sure your key personnel have an assistant they work with who knows the ins and outs of the job, for continuity purposes.

It's wise for you or one of your managers or leaders to connect with newer hires to review the processes and to ask them these three questions:

1. What works about the process?
2. What's not working or what is missing from the process?
3. What would you suggest to make the process even better?

Let them test out their suggestions to see if they help improve the process. If so, have them update the documented process. If not, acknowledge them for trying new things (which so many people resist!) and then discuss going back to the original process or other possible ideas to make the process better. Make sure they act on those changes, so they don't get stuck doing the same thing and expecting better results.

STORE PROCESSES SO YOUR TEAM HAS ACCESS TO THEM

One of the biggest mistakes we've seen when it comes to having documented processes is the team not having access to the files they need, when they need them. You may create beautiful, documented processes that explain every step of how things are done at your company … and then they sit buried in a folder somewhere or in some three-ring binder in your office. If someone is working from home or traveling for business, they can't access a process they need.

Having a clear process written out or on video—and accessible to anyone on your team—is extremely helpful if the person who is currently using that process no longer works at your company or is on vacation. It's also vital for when you hire someone who will be following that time-tested process, or for training someone on your team who can help in a pinch because they already have that training. It gives them a clear starting point, and they can always improve or build on it over time.

Using business process documentation software is another key for sharing files—one that has benefitted our business enormously.

BUSINESS PROCESS DOCUMENTATION SOFTWARE

Business process documentation software can be a game changer for your business, especially when you use it to run your meetings. It allows you to not only store your long-term goals, your annual plan, and your key processes, but it also tracks your weekly to-dos and big quarterly goals for each person on each timeline. It's like a one-stop shop that keeps everyone connected and allows easy, quick reference for your team to find what they need rather than having to look through printed binders or, worse, searching through countless emails to find that one document. It makes your life—and your team's—a whole lot simpler.

Here's how this kind of software can help your business thrive.

- **Keeping your A-team happy:** With everything laid out clearly, your team will feel supported, valued, and less overwhelmed, which means they're more likely to stick around for the long haul.
- **Getting all your knowledge in one spot:** Think of this as your business's brain, storing all your know-how in one place. With

templates that have been tried and tested, you'll be creating and updating processes with ease.

- **Onboarding and training:** Rather than having employees endure boring training sessions, onboarding and training can be a breeze and save you time if you use software. Every role in your company can have its own playbook, making sure everyone knows what they're doing without you having to repeat yourself a million times.
- **Keeping track without the headache:** Want to make sure everyone's doing what they're supposed to? This software can provide tests and reports that keep your team members accountable and ensure your business stays in the flow.
- **Seeing the big picture:** Ever wish you could see how everyone fits together in your business? This software lets you visualize who's doing what, making it much easier to delegate tasks and keep things running smoothly.

Business process documentation software is like a Swiss Army knife for your business. It's all about using one tool to make things simpler, more efficient, and a lot less stressful. Whether you're just starting out or scaling up, using this type of software could be the best move you make for a smooth, successful operation. We use Trainual at RealWealth. Other useful software include Confluence, Lucidchart, Hightail, Scribe, SweetProcess, Pellio, Whale, and many others.

HOW PROCESSES TURN INTO SYSTEMS

The way that processes come together to create systems is similar to the way the human body works. It sounds a bit out there, but stick with us.

Your body is a marvel of interconnected processes that make up different systems that play a vital role in maintaining your health and functionality. In a similar way, your business operates through a complex network of systems and processes, ensuring its growth, sustainability, and efficiency. There are some wild similarities between the systems in your body and those in your business.

For example, the nervous system acts as your body's control center, sending and receiving information to coordinate actions and responses. Management serves as your business's nervous system. Your leaders make decisions based on data received, coordinate activities across your organization, and respond to internal and external stimuli to keep your business on course.

Your circulatory system distributes essential nutrients and oxygen to different parts of your body and removes waste products. This system is vital for sustaining life and ensuring each part of your body functions optimally. Communication processes in your business are like the circulatory system. Information (just like oxygen and nutrients) needs to flow seamlessly throughout your organization. Efficient communication systems ensure that every department receives the information it needs to operate effectively.

Then there's your skeletal system. It provides a framework that supports and shapes your body. It gives form, protects your vital organs, and facilitates movement. The organizational structure of your business is like its skeleton. It defines who reports to whom, roles, and responsibilities, and offers support and shape to your company. Just as your bones grow and adapt, so, too, should the organizational structure evolve with your company's needs.

Your immune system protects the body against diseases and foreign bodies, adapting and learning from every new challenge. Risk management in your business functions as its immune system. It identifies, assesses, and mitigates risks, learning from past experiences to better protect the company's health and longevity.

Seeing your business like the human body makes it easier to understand how all the different processes fit together into separate systems. Each part has its job, and when they all work in harmony, you get one major operating system that's healthy and thriving. That's your business operating system. Cool, right?

WHY SYSTEMS ARE IMPORTANT

Business systems are the bread and butter of your company's success. They keep everything connected; therefore, a hiccup in one spot of your business can cause a domino effect. By knowing how your processes are connected, you'll have more clarity about what's working and what needs attention in your company.

Systems handle things like moving products from A to B, managing employees, keeping track of money, looking after customers, and making sure your business processes run like clockwork.

Your systems also support and encourage better teamwork across different roles and departments in your business. These systems bring different parts of your business—like marketing and sales, or underwriting and acquisitions—together to sing in harmony.

Think of your systems as mission-driven. They're all about helping you stay on track toward the mission you've set for the next several years. They support your specific goals, whether that's making more cash, keeping customers smiling, or making a difference in the world.

HOW TO CREATE A SYSTEM

A system is a combined set of processes that work together to create a consistent result in your business. That result might be for your team, or for your clients and customers.

Building a system starts with building each process, as outlined earlier in this chapter. Once you create the processes that work together to fulfill the outcomes in a specific area of your business, you then package those key processes into a system.

Here's a very simple example:

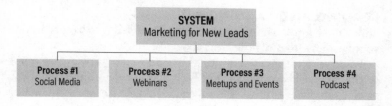

After a system is created and documented, it is vital to ensure it works properly and is easy for your team to access. Again, even the best system isn't going to do much for your company if it sits in a drawer or is buried in multiple foldres on someone's laptop!

You don't have to create all your systems at once. That would be overwhelming and might make you avoid taking any action at all. Instead, have each person on your team take one or two systems to build out each quarter. Have them start with the most important systems that they use on a regular basis. Ask them, "If something happened and you were not able to do your job for ninety days, what are the most important processes we would need to utilize to keep things going in your area of the business?" Their answer can lead you to the first system they need to document, organize, and package into a usable format.

The systems you create will be unique to your business, but we believe there are two systems that are critical for any company: tracking data and using legal systems.

THE IMPORTANCE OF TRACKING DATA

One of the most important systems for your leadership team to utilize is tracking data. Think of data as information, such as facts and numbers, used to analyze things or make decisions. This can be financial numbers, customer information, or employee satisfaction results. Analyzing this data allows you, your leadership team, and just about anyone in your company to better understand how effectively your business is operating and helps you predict where things might be heading. (One of the most effective ways to create and manage this type of system is with business operating system (BOS) software, which we explain in detail in Chapter 13.)

Tracking key numbers doesn't mean just looking at what happened last quarter or last month. You also need to be looking at what is happening in your business today and/or last week to get an idea of where you may end up soon. This is where it's important to understand leading versus lagging numbers.

LEADING AND LAGGING NUMBERS

Think about leading numbers as clues to what's likely to happen next in your business. They're little hints about the future.

For example, think about things like how many new orders you're getting, what's happening in your current market, how much stuff you have in your inventory, or even how confident your customers are feeling about transacting with you.

The reason you want to know your leading numbers is because they help you guesstimate what's coming. They let you tweak your game plan before things happen.

Lagging numbers are all about what's already happened. They're like your business's history book—for example, last quarter's sales, how much profit you made, what you spent, and how happy your customers were with the service they were provided.

Lagging numbers are useful for looking back and understanding what worked and what didn't. They show you the impact of your past decisions.

In simple terms, leading numbers help you prepare for what's next, like you're setting up a weather forecast for your business, while lagging numbers are like looking at last year's weather reports to see what happened. Both are important: One helps you plan for the future, and the other tells you how good your past plans were. It's all about using these insights to make your business smarter and more prepared for whatever comes next!

LEGAL SYSTEMS: DON'T LOSE WHAT YOU'VE BUILT

As you build out systems and processes for your business, make sure to get the advice of experienced and trustworthy professionals. This might include a general business attorney, tax attorney, insurance specialist, real estate broker (if applicable to your business), certified public accountant (CPA), business consultant, financial planner, and any other skilled professional who might provide input on how to utilize time-tested systems and processes and help you protect what you have built.

What disclaimers do you need your customers to understand and sign? What contracts should you be using with your customers or clients? Is your business following the correct standards and procedures for your industry? We hired a California Department of Real Estate attorney to review each process and system we use in our business to make sure we are compliant with the laws of each state we do business in.

As you continue to dial in your systems and processes, remember to ensure you comply with all relevant laws and regulations. We have spoken with many entrepreneurs who wish they had gotten legal advice, which would have helped them avoid lawsuits and compliance issues as it scaled. Not only will great legal counsel help you steer clear of issues, it can also help you keep a lot more of the money you make.

For example, we didn't realize the importance of having an experienced and *creative* tax attorney on our team until over a decade into our business. CPAs are wonderful and necessary, but they often don't have the depth of knowledge in designing your business entities and structures to both protect you and greatly reduce the amount of taxes you pay (legally, of course). A tax attorney can provide significant benefit to your company.

The Dangers of Overdoing Systems and Processes

AJ Osborne, whom we mentioned in Chapter 7, is the CEO of Cedar Creek Capital. As an operator and private owner of over 1.2 million square feet of self-storage, AJ regularly keynotes at national conferences related to self-storage facilities. Here's what he had to say about the potential dangers of systems and processes:

"You can over-process and over-systemize your business, making it mechanical and not moldable. I did that at one time. My company was no longer flexible due to our systems and processes, and our outputs were worse.

"We had created a system for managers to operate our on-site locations. It was very rigid because we were scaling all over the nation. How do you operate a franchise-model business in Pascagoula, Mississippi, and one in Issaquah, Washington, and get the same outcome? I wanted to be like McDonald's—this here, that there, right packaging out. But we did it so much that suddenly, we found out we weren't getting new customers, we were leaving money on the table, and we weren't negotiating. We realized we were so structured, so limited, that our managers and others on the ground were saying no to actual business opportunities.

"We'd created a system that was so rigid, and we got very little feedback. The feedback we did get wasn't coming up from the managers because they thought 'Nope, *this* is the only way we do it, and *this* is how it has to be done.' And then when the markets changed, our systems didn't change and adapt. All of a sudden, we're like, why aren't we executing? We were missing opportunities.

"If you over-systematize and over-process, you can stop growth. Because it's 'We have to follow the system, we can't do that.' 'This is the way we do it.' 'Sorry, this is our policy.'

"Your systems and processes need to be clear, short, and fluid to achieve an objective. They shouldn't be complex and rigid, where you're basically trying to take the human element out of it. You can't do that. You can literally make a ceiling for yourself, and you will miss innovation and opportunities, and you will start to ignore the customer. And you will start to ignore what your business is telling you. Just because it's a process and system doesn't mean it's good.

"As you grow, you need to be flexible on the execution, so you're still getting data that's important to tell you where you need to move. I rely 100 percent on systems and processes, but I will also throw any of them out at any time."

BE OPEN TO MAKING CHANGES

Scaling your business using systems and processes is a journey that takes time. It's an iterative process, and you need to frequently evaluate what you've created. Be open to making changes based on feedback and your evolving business needs. Continue improving things, stay flexible, and include your team, and you'll see your business grow while you're keeping everything running smoothly. Just remember, it's important to strike a balance between growth and sustainability to ensure long-term success *and* keep your sanity.

And to all of you big-idea people out there, please know that when these systems and processes are in place, you become free, not bound. Knowing that all the details of your business are being handled by experts allows you to express your unique strengths, which may be networking, promoting, and ideating. For example, for me (Kathy), once Rich had replaced nearly all the jobs I had been doing with people who were even better at them than I was, I felt a little lost ... until I realized all I had to do was what I loved doing: educating, dealmaking, and networking. It was at that moment I got a call from BiggerPockets, inviting me to cohost their newest podcast, *On the Market*. Shortly after that, they offered me a book deal. And here we are. It could only happen because the details of our business were in very capable hands.

TAKEAWAYS

▶ You want to create *scalable* systems and processes— these will form the infrastructure that help put your business on autopilot mode. But remember, you can't automate everything; you need real people to make big decisions, think of new ideas, and handle customers.

▶ A process is like a company's to-do list for getting stuff done. It's an organized, documented set of tasks that your company does to reach a goal.

▶ A system is a combined set of processes that work together to create consistent results in your business.

▶ Don't create all the systems and processes in your business yourself. Ask the person on your team who is following a certain process to document it and then to help build a system with that process.

▶ Build systems and processes that can be replicated and followed consistently by your team. By creating and organizing a reliable and easy-to-access "holding system," you help ensure everyone on your team can find what they need. Use business process documentation software to assist with this.

- ▶ Don't be overly rigid when following your systems and processes. They are meant to evolve with your business.
- ▶ Use your data, including leading numbers and lagging numbers, to guide you in making changes.
- ▶ Hire a team of experts to help you navigate the legal aspects of your business.

CHAPTER 13

SCALING WITH TECHNOLOGY

The first rule of any technology used in a business is that automation applied to an efficient operation will magnify the efficiency. The second is that automation applied to an inefficient operation will magnify the inefficiency.

—BILL GATES, COFOUNDER, MICROSOFT

Scaling your organization isn't always about working harder—it's about working smarter. In today's rapidly evolving business world, technology is key to being able to do that. It can be your trusty sidekick when it comes to growing more effectively, wowing your customers, and staying ahead of the game. When you make good use of technology, it allows you to unlock your full potential and focus on what you—and your team—are great at.

As we've mentioned before, scaling your business the smart way is more than just a path to financial gain. It's also a way to provide value, focus on your strengths, and have more time to do what you love. Can the smart use of technology in your business help facilitate all of this? Absolutely! We'll show you how in this chapter.

WHY LEVERAGE TECHNOLOGY?

When you leverage technology to streamline your operations and expand your reach, you build a stronger foundation for long-term growth and to generate more revenue. More revenue means you can invest strategically, keep innovating, attract new customers, and tap into new markets.

But there's more to it than just money.

Your team's expertise and unique talents are often what make your business successful. Scaling with technology lets you hand off the everyday tasks to automation and specialized tools, so your team can invest more time into using their strengths and what they excel at. Instead of being swamped with the day-to-day grind of running the business, your team can step back and enjoy the benefits of their hard work. This shift not only reenergizes your team's love for their work, it also empowers them to take on those big, strategic projects that can take your business to new heights.

THERE IS TECHNOLOGY FOR ALMOST EVERYTHING

Whether you're a scrappy start-up or an established corporation, leveraging the right technology can give you an edge. Here are some examples of valuable tech your business can use to scale smart.

CUSTOMER RELATIONSHIP MANAGEMENT (CRM)

Ever heard of Salesforce, HubSpot, or Keap? These CRMs can be your secret weapon for managing your customers and leads. They help you keep track of who's who, automate marketing, and keep you top of mind for your customers. We have been using a CRM in our business from day one. There are dozens of different options out there that you can use (we've tried several over the years and currently use Keap). What matters is that you start getting your customer list into a CRM as soon as possible, so you can take advantage of all the options and benefits. You can always migrate your customer account information into a different CRM later.

E-COMMERCE

E-commerce technology offers easy-to-use tools that make selling stuff online a breeze. They handle everything from inventory management to payments, so you can scale your online store, reach a broader audience, and increase your sales. As of the writing of this book, some of the platforms include Shopify, Wix, Squarespace, and WooCommerce.

Of course, the need for an e-commerce solution is dependent on your industry and/or product. If you own a real estate company, you might not have a need for e-commerce tech. However, it could come in handy if you sell live events, meetups, property tours, courses, mentoring, or masterminds.

ARTIFICIAL INTELLIGENCE (AI) AND MACHINE LEARNING (ML)

Robots might not be taking over *just* yet, but AI and ML are here to help your business grow. Chatbots, recommendation engines, and predictive analytics are great digital helpers that can automate repetitive tasks, help you create content, assist your marketing team, and even predict customer behavior.

The business world is just starting to see the power of AI. It will become a disrupter for many industries and change how we do things. However, for now, remember that AI is a tool to help you rather than something to rely on. AI is still developing and can still be loaded with inaccuracies and create plagiarism in content if you don't use it correctly. You should always fact-check anything generated by AI.

SOCIAL MEDIA MARKETING AND PROMOTION

Facebook, Instagram, X (formerly Twitter), TikTok, and LinkedIn aren't just for silly videos and selfies. They can be powerful tools for marketing your business and increasing sales. You can target who sees your ads, track your impact, and make social media your business buddy. There are numerous platforms (and more popping up all the time) that offer targeted advertising options and analytics tools to help your business reach its ideal audience more effectively.

Social media marketing can also enhance your brand's visibility and customer engagement. With social media being used by more and more people for news, entertainment, and education, it has become what television used to be for businesses—a way to reach more people with your message and your offerings. Learning how to best utilize this powerful marketing tool can be explosive for the future of your brand.

REMOTE COLLABORATION

Zoom, Microsoft Teams, and Slack are currently some of the most popular software programs for keeping everyone in sync, no matter where they're located. These tools can improve productivity, communication, and teamwork, especially in businesses with a remote or distributed workforce.

CLOUD COMPUTING AND STORAGE

Platforms like Amazon Web Services (AWS), Microsoft Azure, and Google Cloud offer scalable computing resources, storage, and data analytics. Your business can easily expand its infrastructure, reduce costs, and improve reliability by migrating to the cloud. When your work is stored "in the cloud," you can easily expand your tech firepower and say goodbye to those pesky server crashes.

PROJECT MANAGEMENT

Imagine you're in the business of building houses and want to take things up a notch. Obviously, constructing a house is not an easy task; it's like putting together a complex puzzle. You've got to follow a specific sequence of steps—for instance, you can't install the windows if you haven't put up sturdy walls. And you've got a whole team of experts, each with their own specialized skills, working on different parts of your project. You have to juggle their schedules, making sure you know when your foundation expert is available, when your tile pro can work their magic, and so on. And what if the weather decides to throw a curveball with some unexpected rain or snow? Your perfectly laid-out schedule goes out the window.

That's where the magic of project management software comes into play. It can manage all the pieces of the puzzle for you, so you can get those houses built. It's like having a smart and organized assistant that helps you keep everything in line, makes sure tasks happen in the right order, and adapts on the fly when things don't go as planned. If you have dreams of scaling up your operations, project management software might just be your secret weapon. There are numerous options out there, including Basecamp, Asana, Monday.com, Trello, Smartsheet, ClickUp, and many more.

With project management software, you avoid cumbersome spreadsheets, time-consuming status meetings, and scattered work across various apps and devices. Instead, you have a centralized hub for all communication, project goals, progress tracking, and file storage. This streamlined approach helps to identify bottlenecks, celebrate achievements, and keep your team on course.

Another great benefit of effective project management is that it eliminates confusion. A well-structured project management system ensures that everyone understands their tasks, deadlines, and collaboration partners. This clarity motivates each team member to take ownership of their responsibilities, resulting in more productive and efficient progress on your goals and projects.

With project management software, you also gain instant visibility into project progress. You no longer need to check in with each team member individually to understand how things are going. Instead, the software provides a comprehensive overview, showing who is responsible for what and if you're on track to meet your deadlines.

Project management software is not just about having a system in place; it's about optimizing that system for maximum efficiency. It will keep your business organized, focused, and poised for growth.

BUSINESS OPERATING SYSTEMS (BOS)

One game-changing solution that's gaining momentum in the business world is cloud-based business operating systems. We've been using one for several years and have loved the results. Our online BOS acts as a centralized hub where our team can track weekly to-dos, prioritize work, and meet deadlines.

BOS software is different from project management software because it's focused on how you run your business week by week rather than tracking progress on a project. It provides a clear view of quarterly goals and upcoming commitments, equipping everyone to handle their weekly tasks more effectively. This heightened visibility helps ensure nothing gets overlooked and reduces the risk of missed deadlines or opportunities.

Another standout feature is how it integrates our company's vision into daily operations. By aligning priorities, tasks, and weekly data analysis with our overarching vision, we can ensure that every action contributes to long-term goals. This alignment helps boost a sense of purpose among employees, driving the company toward success.

Having a BOS platform helps improve accountability within an organization, a crucial need in this age of remote work. It includes each person's quarterly goals, and each week your teams have full insight into the progress toward those goals. Are they on track or off track? That alone is a game changer when it comes to effectiveness and accountability. Even when team members are physically distant, the system allows everyone to stay connected. Through regular conversations and reviews, your leaders can provide valuable feedback to remote workers, ensuring everyone remains aligned with company objectives and individual performance goals.

Beyond improving individual and team productivity, a cloud-based BOS solution also streamlines core business processes. It helps teams stay aware of the most important issues going on in their department, discuss those issues, and solve those issues together as a team. A BOS also helps you track your most important metrics, so you know if you're on course with things like numbers of new clients or customers, sales calls made, income by category, and any other KPIs. This translates to reduced operational costs and overall enhanced efficiency.

RECRUITING, HIRING, AND ONBOARDING

We covered how to find, hire, and train the best people who will help you scale your business in Part III of this book—and thankfully, there is technology to help you with that!

When you dive into the world of tech-powered recruitment and onboarding, you'll find that using recruiting and hiring software packs some powerful benefits. First, it makes your talent search much easier. You can forget about the hassle of copying and pasting job ads to different platforms. With just a few clicks, your job listings can pop up on places like ZipRecruiter, LinkedIn, Indeed, and more. Plus, some of these recruiting tools bring everything together in one easy-to-use dashboard, so no more juggling applications from various job boards.

But that's not all. These tools also help your team evaluate and engage with the top candidates, so you can confidently focus on the right people for your team. You can even create an automatic, step-by-step interview process, making life easier for both you and your candidates. Plus, some of this software comes with personality assessments built in, helping you understand the different candidates applying for your positions.

The best part? You get to customize your hiring process to fit your vibe. You can also tweak your job posts, qualifications, and interview stages easily. This means you can fine-tune your team-building process and grow your business with people who match your culture and have the skills to take your business to the next level.

TRANSCRIPTION

Do you remember the days when secretaries or assistants would take notes during executives' meetings or phone calls, or write notes or letters based on what the "boss" would dictate? Today, there is a new secretary in town who can perform just about all those tasks. It's called a transcription app or software. AI-powered services can automatically generate written transcriptions of virtual meetings. This technology can also capture images from slides shown in a virtual meeting and incorporate them into the meeting notes.

As we prepared for writing this book, we used transcription software during our Zoom meetings to take notes during many of the interviews we did with other business owners. It's a whole lot faster, easier, and less expensive than having a human listen to the recording of an interview and then transcribe it.

DEAL ANALYSIS AND PORTFOLIO MANAGEMENT

This type of technology works wonders for real estate, property management, financial planning, and so much more. For example, having a proper real estate pro forma (a financial projection of rental income and expenses) will make all the difference in your acquisition process.

There are many resources for this; the key is inputting the right numbers into the software. Over the years, we have seen that property sellers conveniently leave out certain metrics in their pro formas to make the cash flow or equity capture larger. Having the right tools in place will save you both time and money.

BiggerPockets has resources for this, including a free rental property calculator (you can find it at www.biggerpockets.com/rental-property-calculator). At RealWealth, we also use DealCheck to help analyze data before purchasing, forecast cash flow and appreciation, and offer ongoing portfolio management.

STOCK INVESTING

There is even technology for investing in the stock market! For example, some businesses use IBM's Watson, an AI system that mimics a team of 1,000 researchers working 24/7 to analyze millions of data points every day. This system continuously uses this data to construct predictive models for about 6,000 U.S. companies and creates a portfolio that is focused on long-term growth.

That's only a partial list of how you can use technology for your business. You can also utilize supply chain management software, cybersecurity solutions, blockchain for recordkeeping, and big data analytics software. This is not just for tech geeks. Staying current with technological advancements and adopting creative, new solutions is key to remaining competitive and successful in today's business world. Become an early adopter; that mindset will pay off big-time.

Scaling with AI: A Tech-Driven Journey to Real Estate Mastery

For the past decade, real estate investor and entrepreneur Nathan Brooks has been using innovative technology to scale his business, Bridge Companies, based in Kansas City, Missouri. He has successfully flipped more than 1,000 properties, and his thriving business operation allows him to give back to his community.

Over the past year, Bridge Companies has embraced AI to simplify operations and amplify their message to a broader audience. "Exploring AI's potential to improve interactions with clients and potential clients is crucial; ignoring this can be detrimental," Nathan says.

His company uses AI in many ways. For example, when someone shows interest in the company's mastermind group, an automated email invitation is sent for the person to provide their details. This information then triggers a sequence that automatically schedules a meeting with Nathan or a team member. If the person joins the mastermind group, AI systems manage their integration by adding them to relevant Facebook groups and events and helping them navigate their membership portal.

From there, clients undergo a tailored sequence of steps based on their responses to an initial survey. This automation ensures they are added to every pertinent calendar event and tagged according to their preferences, goals, and other personal details.

At the core of Nathan's technological lead-flow arsenal is an AI engine that optimizes video content, predicts engagement levels, and posts content with engaging captions automatically. This AI engine not only streamlines content creation, it also keeps Bridge Companies in the public eye. Automation extends to scheduling and client relationship management too, with calendar scheduling tools and a sophisticated CRM that simplifies the customer interaction process from start to finish.

Looking forward, Nathan is enthusiastic about AI's role in further streamlining operations, which will soon include automating routine tasks like message responses and social media management. His team is developing new AI tools that will eventually handle content creation, including blog posts and social media updates. All of this will transform the company's marketing strategies, boost efficiency and customer service, and allow his team to address more complex issues.

"We are continuously exploring how AI can refine our processes, from the initial client contact to ongoing engagement," Nathan says.

DON'T BE OLD AND SLOW

Logan Mohtashami, the lead analyst for real estate data company HousingWire, often says, "Don't be old and slow." What he means by this is if you are relying on old data or old systems, you will lose the race. Technology is evolving constantly, and faster than ever before. In fact, some of the resources we mentioned in this chapter may even become "old and slow" or obsolete by the time you read this book.

Quick changes can be overwhelming when you've become accustomed to a certain way of doing things. But if you and your team are not willing to adapt, your business will soon become less efficient and clunkier compared to your competitors. Technology exists to make our lives easier. If you're using old technology, however, you are making life harder and probably more expensive.

The opposite of "old and slow" is young and quick. It's not news that young people tend to be more aware of new technologies than older people. That's why we believe it's so important to have young people on your team. And remember, those young people become older and may have a hard time adapting to newer technologies. This means you either need to have a constant flow of twenty-somethings on your team or have your current group commit to staying on top of the ever-changing landscape of technology.

HOW TECH CAN MAKE YOUR WORK LIFE EASIER AND LESS EXPENSIVE

Back in 2009, at the beginning of the Great Recession, I (Kathy) partnered with a forty-year veteran developer to pick up foreclosed subdivisions (remember Fred from our partnerships discussion in Chapter 11?). Since bank money was hard to come by at that time, I started syndicating those deals to bring in investor funds.

At RealWealth, we had hired a brilliant tech guy in his twenties to manage our website and CRM. We needed him to build a system for tracking investor funds, investor updates, and distributions. Since syndications were relatively new to us and the digital world, we had to develop the technology ourselves. It was state of the art at the time, and we used it for years.

A decade later, it seemed just about everyone was syndicating. Brand-new investors suddenly owned syndication companies. I wondered how they were able to come up with a system as effective as ours on a small budget.

One day, when I was speaking at a real estate event, I was able to talk with some of those new syndicators to find out how they were managing things. To my surprise, they told me about new software programs we had never heard of that did all the things our system did, without the up-front expenses to build it. It was just subscription-based software that had a fraction of the start-up costs we incurred. After looking at several of the programs, we ditched ours for a newer, shinier version.

This is simply one example of how new technologies can make life easier and cheaper for business owners. But you have to know they exist.

It's easy to get comfortable with your systems, but comfort is the enemy of progress and scaling.

Just remember: You do not have to be the tech genius. You just need someone on your team who is, and you need a team willing to adapt.

Roofstock Soars with Technology

Have you heard of Roofstock? It's an online marketplace for investing in leased single-family homes, mainly for funds to buy in bulk. I (Kathy) met Roofstock's cofounder and CEO, Gary Beasley, when we both won the Goldman Sachs award for 100 Most Intriguing Entrepreneurs in 2012. At the time, Gary was leading his company, Starwood Waypoint Residential Trust, through its IPO. Starwood was one of the first single-family rental platforms, and one of the largest at the time. After Starwood, Gary went on to cofound Roofstock, which has raised $365 million in funding since its inception in 2015 and was valued at $1.9 billion in 2022.

While Gary and I were in the same industry and the same market and had even been recognized for the same award, our company was not valued at $1.9 billion! I had to know—what was his secret?

When I got a chance to interview Gary on the *Real Wealth Show* podcast, in 2023, I asked him how he was able to get Roofstock started with little prior experience in single-family rentals. I, on the other hand, had far more experience, helping thousands of investors build their own rental portfolios nationwide. I'd had the idea to start a fund specifically for the purpose of buying and holding rental property in 2009, but I didn't do it, because I had no idea how to manage such an undertaking.

Gary said he partnered with a tech guy, who was not hard to find in the San Francisco Bay Area. His partner developed a program that could be used on-site with an iPad to quickly search sales comps, rental comps, and the costs of repairs, so they could make quick decisions on acquisitions. While this is common today, it was groundbreaking then.

Literally, the difference between RealWealth being a multimillion-dollar company versus a billion-dollar company was lack of technology. That software allowed Roofstock to scale in a way that their competitors could not.

As we said earlier, RealWealth was at the forefront of many technological advances, like being one of the first to use teleseminars (and then webinars soon after), email funnels, and podcasts, but keeping up with technology changes in all areas is key.

WHAT DOES YOUR BUSINESS NEED?

Tech isn't some fancy add-on—it can be the secret sauce to a thriving business that allows everyone on your team to focus on their unique strengths rather than being bogged down in mundane, repetitive tasks. It's not a matter of trying out the latest craze but of figuring out ways to make your business operations more effective, smoother, and way smarter.

Staying in tune with the latest technology isn't just a good idea—it's essential. Your business needs to evolve with the times and not just keep up, but stand out. The tools we mentioned in this chapter can make the difference between a business that does okay and one that's crushing it.

In essence, smartly integrating technology into your organization is more than a strategy. It's a mindset. It's about embracing change, encouraging a culture of innovation, and tapping into the full potential of your team and your business. As we move through an era where tech is constantly and rapidly changing the game, those who adapt and leverage these advancements will not just survive the market—they'll lead it.

TAKEAWAYS

▶ Using the latest tools and technologies can enhance your efficiency, expand your reach, improve your customers' experiences, and ultimately help you achieve sustainable, smart growth.

▶ Tech helps you not only build a more successful and profitable business, it also provides the priceless gift of time—which can be invested into focusing on things that truly matter.

▶ There is a tech solution for just about everything you can imagine, from project management tools that keep everything running like a well-oiled machine to AI systems that give you the upper hand in marketing, copywriting, and process creation.

▶ Don't be "old and slow"; your business must keep up with the times to succeed in the long run.

▶ Tech can be your MVP in turning challenges into opportunities!

CONCLUSION

You've made it to the end of this book—congratulations! Think about all you've learned.

You know how to build a self-managing business that generates passive income, gives you the freedom you desire, and makes a positive impact on the world. You'll be creating a company that runs on autopilot, so you don't have to spend every waking moment working in your business.

You've learned the differences between growth and scaling, and why it's critical to your long-term survival not to grow too quickly. You know you need to check your ego, be humble, and stay open to learning.

You understand the value of defining your personal "why," so you can create a business that's aligned with your purpose—your personal values, vision, and goals.

You know how to create a business blueprint that includes your business purpose, mission, and vision, and that defining core values for your business is fundamental for success. You also know how to create a company culture where people feel valued and enjoy coming to work.

You have the knowledge to create organizational charts, hire and onboard the best people, and outsource specialists whenever you need to.

You have a new understanding of what personal leadership is, and you can start embodying it. You know how to empower and inspire not just your team leaders but *all* your employees. You get the importance of creating self-managing teams and how to help your team leaders run these teams, and team meetings, effectively.

You've learned about different types of partnerships and how having partners can help you access resources and expertise faster, allowing you to scale faster.

You know that automating your business is essential for efficiency and that using the processes, systems, and technologies in this book will help you get there.

In short, you've learned how to scale your business the smart way.

Now that you've got the tools, and you know how important this stuff is, you can start putting it into practice in your business.

But no one can do everything at once! We've given you a lot to chew on, and we don't want you to get overwhelmed, so implement a little at a time and keep going. Please use this book as a resource and keep returning to it over the years as you continue to scale.

We would love to hear how you're doing with scaling your self-managing business. Feel free to reach out to us through our website at RealWealth.com or on social media.

We can tell you we've walked this path and emerged stronger, wiser, and more successful. We scaled smart—and you can do it too.

This is *your* journey. Keep that entrepreneurial spirit alive. Remember the purpose born from creating something great, serving, and adding value. It's a beautiful reward. Stick with it. The world needs you. The impact you have will make it all worthwhile.

You are making it happen. Don't give up. Keep dreaming and keep scaling.

Now go out there and crush it!

ACKNOWLEDGMENTS

First off, a huge thank you to BiggerPockets Publishing for choosing us to write this book. We know there are many other highly qualified candidates within your membership of over 3 million people, so we are deeply humbled and grateful for the opportunity to share our story.

Massive thanks to you, Savannah Wood, for your positive attitude, your valuable feedback, and constant encouragement. We can see why BP Publishing chose you as an inspiring leader. And, of course, high fives to the whole team at BiggerPockets for welcoming us into your "family" and for the massive positive impact you are having on the real estate and business community.

Melissa Brandzel, you rock! This book is so much better thanks to your incredible editing and writing skills. We clicked from day one, and that connection only got better over time.

We want to extend our appreciation to every business leader who was willing to share their insights, ideas, and stories with our readers: Nathan Brooks, Dan Coleman, Jilliene Helman, Ken McElroy, AJ Osborne, Kevin Rosenbloom, Vicky Schiff, Brian Scrone, Lisa Song-Sutton, Elaine Stageberg, Scott Trench, Brandon Turner, Eric Upchurch, and Tarl Yarber. Your valuable input will help the thousands of other business leaders who read this book and take action on the ideas.

A big shout-out to the thousands of members of RealWealth for being an integral part of our network. Your eagerness to learn, invest, and live life on your own terms benefits not only you and your family but also anyone who reads this book.

Thanks to our whole team at RealWealth for all you have done to help us live our purpose and achieve our mission. That includes every employee, contractor, and all the amazing property teams around the country who take such good care of RealWealth investors.

To our incredible daughters, Karina and Krista, thank you for all the love you bring to our lives. You've both trained us well on how to become better parents, which we believe has helped us to be more understanding, caring, and wise business leaders. Patrick and Alec, thank you for loving our girls and expanding our family (hint hint … more grandbabies, please!).

And finally, thanks to you, the entrepreneur who just completed this book. You obviously care about learning, growing, and building a purpose-driven business that makes a positive difference in the world. By scaling your business, you're doing more than just making money and creating jobs; you are a catalyst for economic growth, impacting families and communities locally, across the country, and around the world. We wish you the best on your journey of growing a business while living a fun, fulfilling life.

RICH

I am grateful for you, Katherine, my caring, talented, and gorgeous wife. Our three decades of love, fun, adventure, passion, support, and belief have been the greatest blessing I could ever ask for. Thank you for being such an amazing human, best friend, lover, co-parent, and business partner. It was such an honor to write this book with you. As I said from the day I met you, "Who could promise me heaven, when heaven's already here?"

To my mom, Mari Fettke: Thanks for always believing in me and supporting all my business ventures—from the haunted house setup in your basement when I was in grade school to co-signing on the big business loan for my gym when I was in my early twenties. You have always been my true angel investor.

Finally, I would like to acknowledge entrepreneurship. Throughout my life, it has challenged me to consistently learn, grow, serve, deal with fear and setbacks, and be more present, while also creating a bigger and better vision of the future.

KATHY

Rich, the day I met you, you looked at me and said, "Haven't I met you before?" And I said, "No, I don't think so," but secretly I thought, *I wish!* Well, it took thirty years to find you, but when I did, the trajectory of my life took a brand-new direction.

I was afraid to speak in public, so you encouraged me to do Toastmasters. Within a year, I was speaking at a convention. I was afraid to go on national television, but you coached me on how to breathe through the fear. I managed to survive each show without fainting. I was afraid to hire and fire employees, and you coached me through the process. Now we have a team of inspired people who care deeply about the role they play in making a difference in the lives of our RealWealth members. Outside of work, I have bungee jumped off bridges, jumped out of airplanes, rock climbed steep cliffs, skied double-black-diamond tree runs, and surfed overhead waves, all because of your encouragement.

There is no doubt I am stronger every day because of you, and life would not be so exciting without you. I'm thrilled we get to enjoy yet another adventure, writing this book together. Now, we can write another book about the things we learned along the way and how we are able to love each other even more after all the hard work. You are my twin flame, and together we burn brighter.

ABOUT THE AUTHORS

Rich Fettke is a licensed real estate broker, active investor, and cofounder of RealWealth.com, a real estate investment group that helps its 75,000+ members improve their financial intelligence, secure passive income from quality investment properties, and obtain financial freedom.

Rich is author of the best-selling book *The Wise Investor: A Modern Parable About Creating Financial Freedom and Living Your Best Life*. He's also the author of *Extreme Success* and the audiobook *Momentum*.

A pioneer in the field of business and personal coaching, Rich is a former vice president of the International Coaching Federation (ICF) and holds one of the ICF's first Master Certified Coach credentials. His work has been featured on TV, radio, and in print, including *USA Today, Entrepreneur Magazine, Inc. Magazine*, and the *Wall Street Journal*.

Kathy Fettke is cofounder of RealWealth and has been a frequent guest expert on CNBC, Fox, ABC, CBS MarketWatch, and Bloomberg for her thoughts on the state of the real estate market.

Kathy is the author of the #1 bestseller *Retire Rich with Rentals* and host of two long-running RealWealth podcasts: *The Real Wealth Show* and *Real Estate News for Investors*. More recently, you'll find her as a cohost on BiggerPockets's *On the Market* podcast.

She was named one of the Top 100 Most Intriguing Entrepreneurs by Goldman Sachs two years in a row for her work in helping solve the foreclosure crisis.

Kathy and Rich live in Malibu, California, where they invest, work, and play together.

ADDITIONAL RESOURCES

BOOKS

Traction: Get a Grip on Your Business by Gino Wickman

Extreme Ownership: How U.S. Navy SEALs Lead and Win by Jocko Willink and Leif Babin

Beyond Entrepreneurship: Turning Your Business into an Enduring Great Company by James Collins and William C. Lazier

Mastering the Rockefeller Habits: What You Must Do to Increase the Value of Your Growing Firm by Verne Harnish

Scaling Up: How a Few Companies Make It…and Why the Rest Don't by Verne Harnish

Vivid Vision: A Remarkable Tool for Aligning Your Business Around a Shared Vision of the Future by Cameron Herold

WEBSITES

BelaySolutions.com—For hiring virtual assistants, bookkeepers, and accounting professionals

StrategicCoach.com—Dan Sullivan's Strategic Coach® program for growth-minded entrepreneurs

BiggerPockets.com—For real estate investors and professionals who want education, tools, and a community of more than 2 million members, all in one place

EOSWorldwide.com/eos-model—Gino Wickman's Entrepreneurial Operating System® (EOS)

RealWealth.com—For busy business owners who want to passively invest some of their profits into growing a real estate portfolio

U.S. Chamber of Commerce—The Chamber's CO website is full of helpful education and resources for small business owners (https://www.uschamber.com/co/)

REFERENCES

Arguinchona, Joseph H., and Prasanna Tadi. "Neuroanatomy, Reticular Activating System." StatPearls Publishing. July 24, 2023. https://www.ncbi.nlm.nih.gov/books/NBK549835/.

"Atomic." *The Oxford Pocket Dictionary of Current English.* Encyclopedia.com. https://www.encyclopedia.com/science-and-technology/physics/physics/atomic#atomic.

Bautner, Alison. "One-on0one with 'Woz': Steve Wozniak talks Steve Jobs." *The Milwaukee Business Journal.* June 27, 2014. https://www.bizjournals.com/milwaukee/blog/2014/06/one-on-one-with-woz-steve-wozniak-talks-steve-jobs.html.

"Business Employment Dynamics." U.S. Bureau of Labor Statistics. April 28, 2016. https://www.bls.gov/bdm/entrepreneurship/entrepreneurship.htm.

Chamberlain, Andrew. "What Matters More to Your Workforce than Money." *Harvard Business Review.* January 17, 2017. https://hbr.org/2017/01/what-matters-more-to-your-workforce-than-money.

"Inspire." *Merriam-Webster Dictionary.* https://www.merriam-webster.com/dictionary/inspire.

Jackson, Sarah. "'Activate the Space': WeWork Founder Adam Neumann Made Staff Sit at Empty Desks, Throw Parties, and Play The Notorious B.I.G. When Investors Toured Buildings, New Book Says." *Business Insider.* July 20, 2021. https://www.businessinsider.com/wework-staff-throw-parties-fill-empty-desks-cult-of-we-2021-7.

Nightingale, Earl. *The Strangest Secret.* https://edisciplinas.usp.br/pluginfile.php/5585445/mod_resource/content/1/16Earl_Nightingale_The%20Strangest%20Secret-Nightingale.pdf

Parker, Will, and Konrad Putzier. "Houston Apartment Owner Loses 3,200 Units to Foreclosure as Multifamily Feels the Heat." *The Wall Street Journal.* April 11, 2023. https://www.wsj.com/articles/houston-apartment-owner-loses-3-200-units-to-fore-closure-as-multifamily-feels-the-heat-fb3d0e75.

Sidders, Jack. "Blackstone Reaches Deal With Bondholders on Defaulted Nordic Debt." *Bloomberg.* December 15, 2023. https://www.bloomberg.com/news/articles/2023-12-15/blackstone-reaches-deal-with-bondholders-on-defaulted-nordic-debt.

Styr, Caroline. "5 Things That Make Workers Stay at Their Jobs (Hint: It's Not Salary)." World Economic Forum. December 15, 2022. https://www.weforum.org/agenda/2022/12/5-things-that-make-workers-stay-at-their-jobs-not-salary/.

"The Future of Work Beyond the Pandemic: Takeaways from our Global Workforce of the Future Report." The Adecco Group. September 27, 2022. https://www.adeccogroup.com/future-of-work/latest-insights/the-future-of-work-beyond-the-pandemic#.

"The State of Veteran Homelessness." U.S. Department of Veterans Affairs. 2022. https://www.va.gov/HOMELESS/State-of-Veteran-Homelessness-2022.pdf.

Truong, Kevin. "San Francisco's Biggest Landlord Defaulted on a Massive Loan." *The San Francisco Standard*. January 13, 2023. https://sfstandard.com/2023/01/13/san-franciscos-biggest-landlord-defaulted-on-a-massive-loan/.

Wadhwa, Vivek, Krisztina Holly, Raj Aggarwal, and Alex Salkeve. "Anatomy of an Entrepreneur: Family Background and Motivation." *Kauffman Foundation Small Research Projects Research*. July 8, 2009. https://www.kauffman.org/reports/the-anatomy-of-an-entrepreneur/.

Wong, Belle. "What Is Company Culture? Definition & Development Strategies." *Forbes Advisor*. August 15, 2023. https://www.forbes.com/advisor/business/company-culture/.

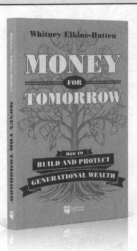
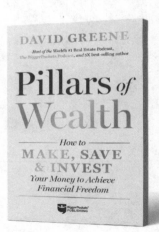

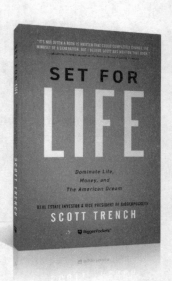
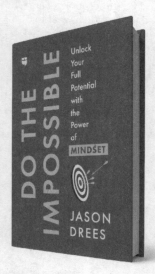

6 Steps to 7 Figures: A Real Estate Professional's Guide to Building Wealth by Pat Hiban

All the tactics that the best real estate agents use to become financially free and pursue the lives of their dreams.

www.biggerpockets.com/6steps

Real Estate Partnerships: How to Access More Cash, Acquire Bigger Deals, and Achieve Higher Profits
By Ashley Kehr and Tony Robinson

Real estate investing can be a complicated puzzle—you need time, money, experience, and connections to start and scale your business effectively. Rather than hustling to provide every component on your own, finding a real estate partner can help fast-track you to the portfolio of your dreams.

www.biggerpockets.com/partnerships

Looking for more?
Join the BiggerPockets Community

BiggerPockets brings together education, tools, and a community of more than 2+ million like-minded members—all in one place. Learn about investment strategies, analyze properties, connect with investor-friendly agents, and more.

Go to **biggerpockets.com** to learn more!

 Listen to a **BiggerPockets Podcast**

 Watch **BiggerPockets on YouTube**

 Join the **Community Forum**

 Learn more on **the Blog**

 Read more **BiggerPockets Books**

 Learn about our **Real Estate Investing Bootcamps**

 Connect with an **Investor-Friendly Real Estate Agent**

 Go Pro! Start, scale, and manage your portfolio with your **Pro Membership**

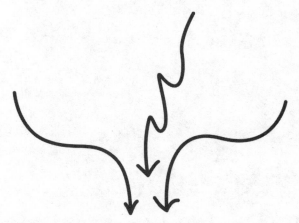

Follow us on social media!

Sign up for a Pro membership
and take **20 PERCENT OFF**
with code **BOOKS20**.